D0383093

■ From Castle to Teahouse

▪ FROM CASTLE

JAPANESE ARCHITECTURE OF THE

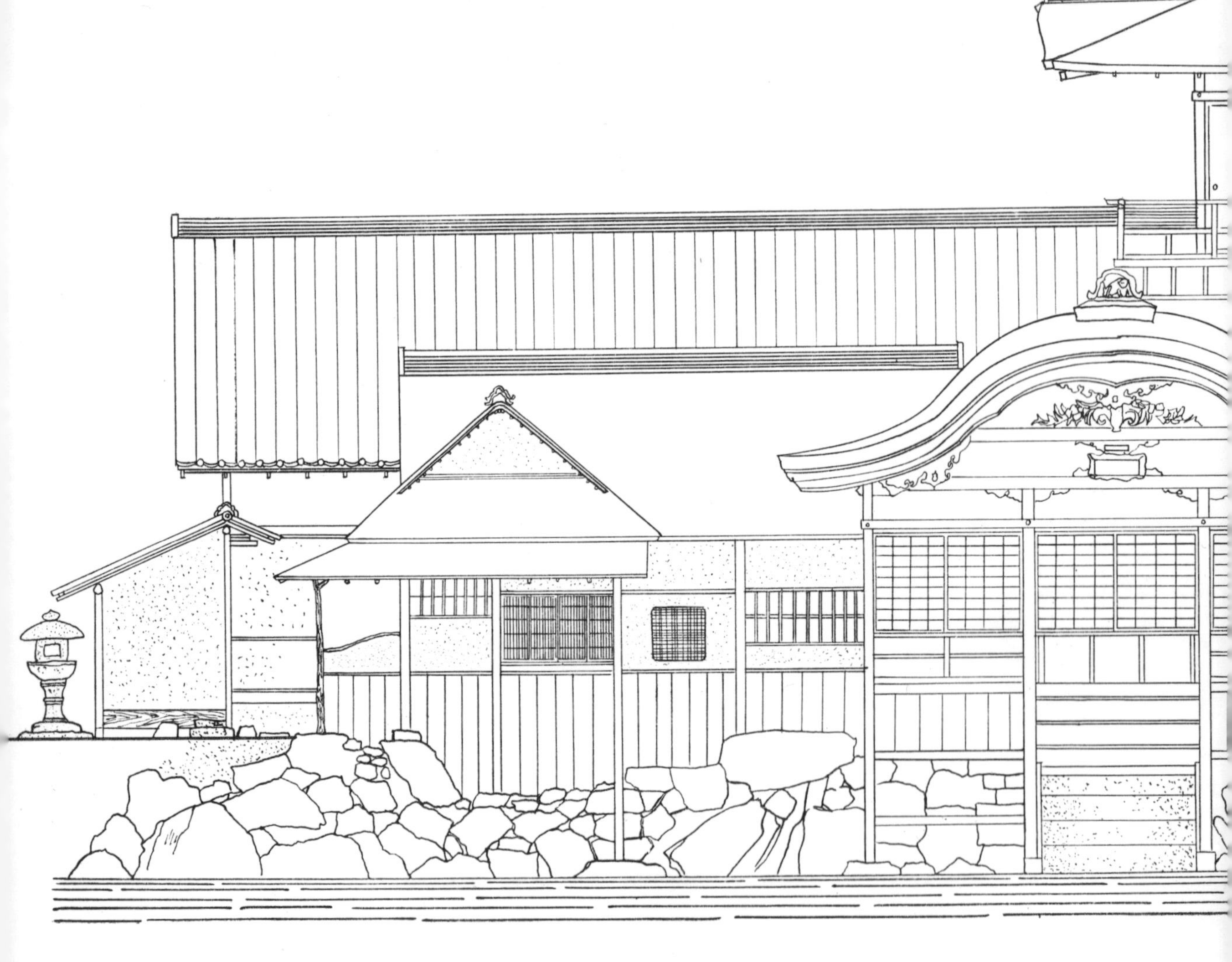

FROM CASTLE TO TEAHOUSE

JAPANESE ARCHITECTURE OF THE MOMOYAMA PERIOD

John B. Kirby, Jr.

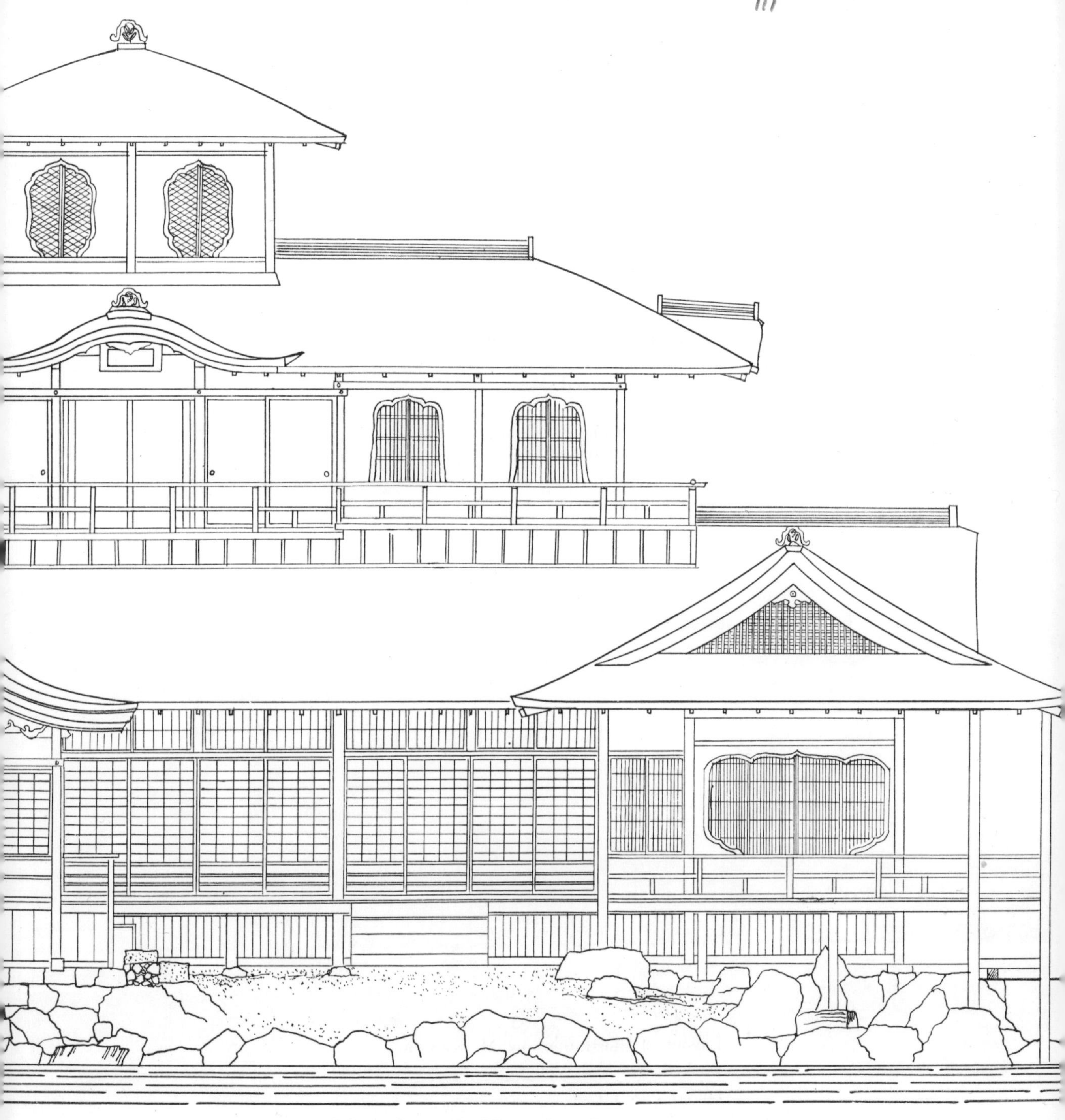

RUTLAND, VERMONT: Charles E. Tuttle Company: TOKYO, JAPAN

European Representatives
For the Continent:
BOXERBOOKS, INC., Zurich
For the British Isles:
PRENTICE-HALL INTERNATIONAL, INC., London

Published by the Charles E. Tuttle Company,
of Rutland, Vermont & Tokyo, Japan
with editorial offices at
15 Edogawa-cho, Bunkyo-ku, Tokyo

Library of Congress Catalog
Card No. 62–9361

First edition, 1962

Layout of illustrations by M. Kuwata
Book design and typography by Kaoru Ogimi
PRINTED IN JAPAN

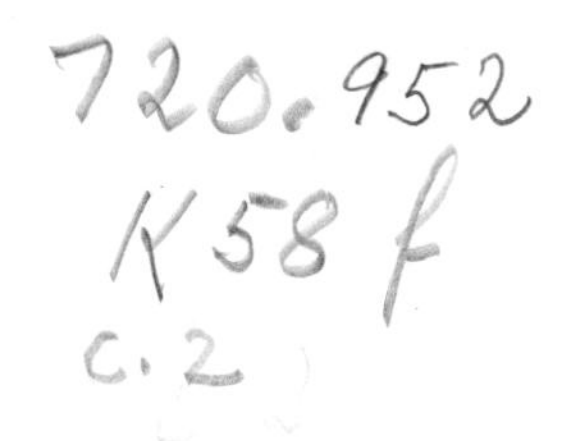

To Jan

Contents

List of Illustrations

PART ONE: The Forms

PART TWO: Representative Examples

Foreword

■ *THE MOMOYAMA period of Japanese art history—1573 to 1615—offers such a variety of architectural pleasures that, in at least one of its many facets, it should appeal to every taste. It ranges from the largest and most imposing castles and palaces to the smallest and most tastefully designed teahouses. Painting and gardens are an integral part of Japanese architecture and here, also, the range extends from the gorgeous and elaborate to the utmost in simplicity and restraint.*

In contrast to other eras, the architectural developments of the Momoyama period were not chiefly concerned with the building of religious edifices. During this time of conquest and consolidation in which the Japanese nation came to be united under a single leader, military architecture was of prime importance. More important in terms of application to contemporary design was the shoin *style of residential architecture, which reached its zenith in this period of creativity. The third major architectural contribution of the age was the introduction of the* sukiya *style, represented by the teahouse. It is indeed remarkable that in such a short period of time these three dissimilar but related types of architecture developed forms which have never been surpassed in Japan or, in the opinion of many, in the world.*

The shoin and sukiya styles have left their imprint on Japanese residential architecture, which retains many of the forms of the Momoyama period to this day. Therefore a knowledge of the influence of these styles is pertinent to a study of contemporary Japanese architecture and the latter's impact upon the rest of the modern world.

In the first part of this book I have discussed and illustrated the principal forms of castle, shoin, and sukiya architecture which I feel were the most important contributions of the period. The second part consists of existing examples of Momoyama structures followed by a brief section on developments of less importance in religious architecture and construction of essentially an engineering nature.

I have tried to keep the text as untechnical as possible. The approach is that of an architectural historian using a minimum of architectural terms and including pertinent historical data. I have also tried to limit the number of Japanese words in the text. English explanations follow all but the more obvious terms. Should there be doubt, English explanations of all Japanese terms appear in the index as also do the long-vowel marks for Japanese words.

It is hoped that through an understanding of forms and examples from this creative period of Japanese history, the reader will appreciate the heritage of Japan's architectural past and the background upon which are based her aspirations for the future.

The kindness of many people both in Japan and in America has made this book possible. I am indebted to all Japanese for letting me visit their beautiful country and study their architectural treasures. I particularly wish to thank the owners and caretakers of temples, shrines, castles, and teahouses for the permission to photograph their buildings.

I wish also to express appreciation to the many persons who have spent time and effort which contributed to this volume. I am indebted to Ambassador Toshikazu Kase, who helped my wife and me in planning our trip to Japan. We were very fortunate in being "adopted" by the Yojibei Yoshikawa family of Fushimi, in Kyoto, and their loving care and companionship will always be gratefully remembered. I must thank Miss Utako Miyaki, who accompanied me on most of my photographic adventures; she acted as an interpreter, and her knowledge of Japanese courtesies (almost ritualistic at times) was an aid in securing admission to many examples of architecture. The late Mr. Jiro Kato, an authority on the Fushimi-Momoyama area and Fushimi Castle, conferred with me often concerning his field, and his passing was a great personal loss. I owe a great debt to Mr. Tomoya Masuda, my teacher in the Department of Architecture of Kyoto University, for his advice, encourage-

ment, and aid. Yoshichiro Marutani is to be thanked for the skill with which he processed my photographs. I also wish to acknowledge the help of Hidesaburo Suzuki of the Kyoto American Cultural Center.

I am indebted to the Nishi Hongan-ji of Kyoto for Figures 89–111 and to an anonymous friend for Figures 115–32 on Nijo Castle. Figure 177 is reproduced from Nihon no Kenchiku *by permission of the authors, Hirotaro Ota, Tai Tanabe, and Katsukichi Hattori. All other photographs in the book are my own work.*

I am grateful to students of the Department of Architecture of Kyoto University for all the line drawings in this book. Figure 46 is from a plan by Junichi Tsuchiya, who in turn acknowledges his indebtedness to a publication entitled "Azuchi-jo Tenshu Fukugenko, Rombun-shu No. 1"; and Figures 12 and 13 are based upon models made by Masabumi Oshima. I also wish to thank my father for the loan of a camera and my wife for enduring the travels and sacrifices that a work of this nature entailed.

JOHN B. KIRBY JR.

■ PART ONE
The Forms

■ *ALTHOUGH the Momoyama period lasted for only forty-two years, from 1573 to 1615, the dynamic events that occurred at this time make it the most exciting and interesting era in Japanese history. This period saw the unification of the country and the invasion of Korea by Hideyoshi's forces. It was most profoundly influenced by the Europeans who had arrived in 1542 and introduced firearms and Christianity to Japan. Paralleling these major events was the development of architectural forms very different from those employed at any other time or place in the world. It was a period of prosperity, of commercial contact with Asia and Europe, and of national unity that provided Japan's rulers with the power to build on a large and impressive scale.*

The Momoyama period was dominated by three military leaders. Oda Nobunaga (1534–82) began the cycle by bringing a large part of the country under his power. His Azuchi Castle on the shores of Lake Biwa introduced advanced military architecture combined with palatial living quarters on a large and lavish scale. Nobunaga was assassinated in 1582 and was succeeded by Toyotomi Hideyoshi (1536–98). Hideyoshi is probably Japan's favorite military hero, and the fact that he was of peasant origin makes his rise to power all the more amazing. Hideyoshi died in 1598 while his troops were still attempting unsuccessfully to subjugate Korea. His Fushimi Castle, which was later called Momoyama Castle, gave its name to this period of history.

THE FORMS 2

The third great leader was Tokugawa Ieyasu (1542–1616), who controlled the country after Hideyoshi's death, although his position was challenged until the death of Hideyoshi's son, Hideyori, in the final siege of Osaka Castle in 1615. Ieyasu was the first of a long line of Tokugawa shoguns (military rulers) who remained in power until 1868.

Because of unstable military conditions, castles played an important part in the architecture of the Momoyama period. However, within the castles other forms of architecture developed. The large-sized fortifications demanded equally large buildings within the castle compounds. For the castle owner, huge buildings in the shoin style served this purpose, and smaller structures in the same style were utilized for nobles and generals. In this period the tea ceremony, which had previously been introduced from China, became popular with people of all social classes. Sen no Rikyu, Japan's greatest tea master, was instrumental in the development of an architectural style devoted solely to the tea ceremony, and the forms of the teahouse set a new architectural mode called sukiya. Hideyoshi patronized the tea ceremony and often retired from his huge elaborate buildings to the quiet simplicity of the small teahouses located within the walls of his castle.

Before examining the existing examples of Momoyama architecture, it is necessary to become familiar with the principal forms of castle, shoin, and sukiya architecture, which are discussed in the succeeding chapters.

■ I
The Castle

■ THE NEED for protection against aggression has been a problem for men of all countries. In Japan, from the beginning of recorded history there has been mention of primitive fortifications designed to lessen vulnerability to enemy attacks. Earth, stone, and wooden walls; holes, ditches, moats, and natural barriers were the principal forms employed from early times. The fortified residence is probably the forerunner of the castle. In areas where there were large military organizations, the residences of the leaders and their supporting troops had to be strongly protected. In the two centuries preceding the rise of Nobunaga, central Japan was divided and ruled by numbers of warlords. The struggles among them brought about the further development of military architecture through the construction of larger fortresses capable of withstanding sieges by a greater number of men.

As Nobunaga gained control of large sections of the country, it became possible for him to build a castle of appreciable size and complexity. Such castles, of ever-increasing strength, continued to be built throughout the Momoyama period, and it was not until the country became completely unified and peaceful under the Tokugawas that the importance of the castle began to decline.

There are three distinct castle types, classified according to their topographic location: the *sanjo* or castle located at the summit of a small mountain; the *hirajo,* located on a plain; and the *hirasanjo,* located partly on a mountain and partly on a plain. The sites chosen for castles were strategic positions, often close to the sea or rivers in order to facilitate shipping and at the same time provide protection. The advantages of the mountain castle were that it gave a view of the surrounding

1. Main and Subsidiary Towers (Tenshukaku and Shotenshu). The main tower, the highest and largest building of the castle, was used for observation and as a command post for military activities. *Himeji Castle*

2. Moat (Hori). In Japan, as elsewhere in the world, moats played an important defensive role in military architecture. *Osaka Castle*

3. Rampart across the Moat (Dobashi). Since the dobashi were guarded by gate towers, attacking forces using them were vulnerable to heavy fire. *Nijo Castle*

4. Corner Tower (Sumi-yagura). This type of tower, usually of two or three stories, was designed primarily for observation and for defense of corner sections.

Osaka Castle

5. Wall Building (Tamon). The tamon, whose outer side served as part of the castle wall, was used for storage and was entered from the inner side.

Himeji Castle

6. Wall Openings for Weapons (Sama). Openings in the castle walls served for firing upon the enemy, the shape of the aperture varying with the weapon used. *Himeji Castle*

7. Tower Gate (Watariyagura). This combination gate and tower provided an enclosed passage above the gate for crossing from one compound to another or firing upon the enemy. *Himeji Castle*

8. Gables: Triangular (Chidori-hafu) and Curved (Karahafu). A combination of these two gable types breaks up the mass of the large castle towers.
Wakayama Castle

9. Dolphin Roof Ornaments (Shachi). Tile or metal roof ornaments of this type were supposed to guard against evil.
Osaka Castle

10. Trap Doors for Dropping Stones (Ishiotoshi). This device served to protect vulnerable corner sections against enemy forces trying to climb the walls. *Wakayama Castle*

11. Windows: Vertical Slat Type (Renjimado) and Bell-shaped (Katomado). Windows of this type provided sufficient ventilation without sacrificing cover. *Himeji Castle*

area for reconnaissance, that it was relatively inaccessible to attackers, and that it was more likely to survive earthquakes, which are less destructive on the heights than on the plains. The disadvantages were the difficulty of building, the inconvenience of location, the problem of digging wells, and the vulnerability to typhoon winds. The castle on the plain, however, had the disadvantage of being subject to inundation. Takamatsu Castle, for example, owed its impregnability to the surrounding water until Hideyoshi used this very factor to destroy it. A large dike was raised, and the river was diverted into the moat. When the rainy season started, Takamatsu Castle was flooded and fell to Hideyoshi's forces. The combination of the castle on the mountain and the plain was most often employed in the Momoyama period since it combined the advantages of the other types.

The plan of the fortress consisted of a number of fortified compounds. Within an individual compound there were three types of buildings: those used for combat, residence, and storage. A castle plan was made up of concentric compounds isolated from each other by ramparts, moats, or walls. The central compound contained the main tower and the residences of the most important inhabitants, while the outer ones made up the defensive positions. The magazine was usually located in the second compound. The number and the design of the compounds varied, but there were usually three to five. Round forms were seldom used because they were easier to attack than to defend. In the castle on the plain and mountain, the main compound was set on the elevation. The terrain of the castle on the plain was broken up by moats filled with water or by a river or a lake.

The compounds or courts of a castle had the general name of *kuruwa*. The main compound was called the *hommaru;* the second, the *ni no maru;* and the third, the *san no maru*. In larger castles there were also outer courts. When the plan was irregular, the compounds were given the names of compass directions, people, or significant features. The compounds were located so that if any line of defense was captured, it could be recovered from another line. The courts were connected in labyrinth fashion to make total capture difficult.

The first procedure in building a castle was to lay out ropes on the site marking off the significant features of the plan. This preliminary was known as *nawabari* or marking with ropes. Intricate scaffolding was used in the construction of the castle buildings and walls. Ramps supported by scaffolding were used to transport building materials to the highest sections of the castle towers. Even today the Japanese employ similar methods in the construction of their tall buildings. No nails are used in this scaffolding; the poles are merely tied together with rope.

The building of castles employed many workmen of all sorts, and the protection afforded by the castles, together with the activity centering about them, led to the development of many thriving cities. Tokyo, Osaka, and Nagoya, for example, owe their importance originally to the construction of castles.

For protecting the approaches to a castle, three types of excavation were used: areas filled with water, wide ditches, and tracts of mud or swamp. Of these, the water-filled moat or *hori* afforded the best guarantee against penetration. There were two basic types of moat profile: the U shape, in which the walls on both sides met and supported each other, and the box shape, in which the bottom was flat and the walls were independent of each other. Earthen ramparts called *dobashi* were placed across the moat at points where attackers attempting to cross them would be most vulnerable. Wooden bridges were also used to span moats, and sometimes a combination of rampart and bridge was employed. The largest and most heavily fortified moat surrounded the main compound.

The stone walls so characteristic of the Japanese castle were built on a foundation of earth covered with small stones over which were placed the larger surface stones. Except at the corners, which were fashioned of stone slabs arranged much like the corner of a brick wall, the stones were of no uniform size or pattern. Generally, however, they were wedge-shaped and were placed with the smaller end of the wedge at the surface and the larger on the inside. This arrangement held them locked in position by their own weight and made them resistant to earthquakes. It also necessitated giving the wall a curve, and records show that this was geometrically determined. The basic earthen wall was known as a *doi* and the finished wall of stone as an *ishigaki*. Since no mortar was used to hold the stones in place, free drainage of water was permitted. Nevertheless, openings for drainage were used, although they were kept small so as not to be of advantage to the enemy.

The main gate to the outside of a castle, called the *otemon,* was one of the strongest of the castle gates and was heavily protected. On the opposite side of the castle was the *karamete* or rear gate, through which prisoners were usually taken in and which was sometimes used by the defenders as a point of exit for an attack on the enemy.

The *masugata* was a type of double gate which proved to be very effective and was extensively used in castle architecture. It consisted of two sets of gates with a fixed enclosure between. The secondary door was situated at right angles to the first. *Masu* is the name for a square measuring vessel in Japanese. The advantages of the "measuring gate" were many: the enemy was not able to view the interior of the castle; men could enter or leave without having both gates open at the same time; attackers who gained entrance through the main gate were extremely vulnerable to fire while trying to enter the secondary gate; leaders could also inspect their men in this quarter. The space was fixed by Hideyoshi so that it would hold 240 men or 40 mounted cavaliers.

Strategic gates were constructed of large timbers often protected with plating of copper or iron. These important military points were always guarded by towers from which the enemy could be fired upon.

Castle towers, generically known as *yagura,* derived their specific names from their position or use. Corner towers, for example, were called *sumiyagura.* In exterior appearance they were structures of two or three stories, but the interior was divided into many levels, the topmost of these being used for observation. Since corners hampered lateral observation and provided cover for enemies, it was important that these sectors be protected.

The *tamon,* a long, low structure integrated into the castle wall, was ordinarily used for storage. On the inner side, it had doors leading to the castle compounds; on the outer, openings from which the enemy could be fired upon. Such structures were often built with a gate, and the combination was called a *watariyagura.* The arrangement provided a protected passageway directly above the gate, convenient both for crossing from one part of the castle compound to another and for shooting down upon hostile invaders. This type of tower-gate was frequently constructed as the inner part of a "measuring gate."

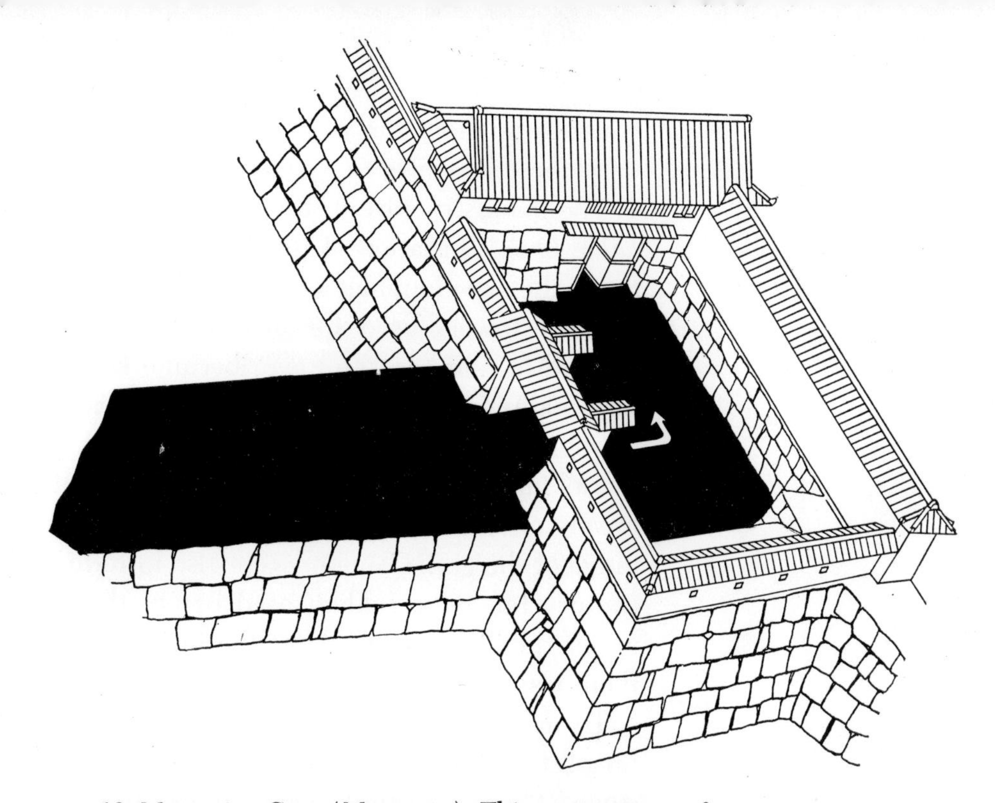

12. Measuring Gate (Masugata). This arrangement of two gates with an enclosure between provided a double line of defense.

Other towers were used for observation, for confining prisoners, and for protecting water supplies. Towers also served for such interesting purposes as moon viewing and committing suicide.

All towers, gate structures, and upper walls were furnished with openings for firing upon attacking forces. These openings, known under the general name of *sama,* were of such specific types as *yasama* for arrows, *tepposama* for guns, and (although rarely) *taihosama* for cannons. The holes provided for arrows were rectangular, while those for guns were circular, triangular, or square. At the end of the Tokugawa period, when the use of firearms had become common, it was necessary to have three openings for guns to every one for bows and arrows.

The tops of walls not protected by other structures were usually occupied by palisades behind which trees were planted in the hope of stopping projectiles, as a means of camouflage, and as a device for concealing activities within the castle. Pine trees were most abundantly represented, since they provided cover throughout the year. Bamboo was grown for arrows and oaks for the shafts of spears.

The main structure or tower of a castle is called the *tenshu-kaku.* One translation of this is "guardian of the sky." We can trace the development of the main tower back to the early wooden towers used for observation. As military forces increased in number, the tower became larger and stronger and eventually came to house the military leader. With the introduction of the Tanegashima or matchlock gun by the Portuguese in 1542, it became necessary to build much stronger towers and to increase the size relative to the ever-increasing range of the gun. Cannons were also introduced late in the 16th century but were seldom used before the country was united under the Tokugawas. After the imposition of Tokugawa rule, there was no longer any occasion for their use.

To achieve elevation and to protect the main tower from fires set by enemy invaders, the rectangular base was built of stone. The supporting beams of the tower rested upon large stones on top of this base or in a cellar within the base. This constituted a departure from many other large examples of Japanese or Chinese architecture in which the beams were sunk in the ground. These bottom posts extended through several floors to a platform which supported the beams for the higher floors. Similar platforms added different levels around the perimeter of the structure. There were usually one or two extremely long posts which might extend from the bottom to the top of the tower for the purpose of giving stability to the different platforms. This structural device, however, should not be compared with the central beam of the pagoda, which is sunk into the ground and is primarily for support. Curved beams were used freely in the framework.

The room at the top of the main tower was often the most luxurious in the castle. It was floored with *tatami* mats and served as the post of the castle lord in time of siege. Because it functioned as an observation point, it was largely open on all four sides and was thus well lighted, well ventilated, and relatively comfortable. At the beginning of the Momoyama period, this observation floor jutted out from the tower roof, but in later castles it was contained within the gradual tapering of the tower outline. It was often surrounded by a balcony with a wooden railing and sometimes adorned with a bell-shaped window called a *katomado*. The principal window style in most castles was of the *renji* type, which consisted of vertical slats in a rectangular frame. This type of window provided good ventilation for the buildings, furnished sufficient protective cover, and afforded openings from which fire could be directed upon the enemy.

The covering for all walls except those made of stone was a type of plaster. Up to the time of Hideyoshi, the exterior walls were painted with a compound whose chief ingredient was persimmon juice. This served both as an insect repellent and as a protection against weathering. A later development was the addition of a lime covering that gave greater protection against fire and offered more resistance to projectiles. The Tokugawas used a tilelike covering of fired earth.

The walls, towers, and gates were usually topped with rows of alternately inverted, semicircular, overlapping tiles, the row at the outer edge consisting of round tiles bearing the crest of the castle owner. A lime mortar made the joints waterproof, gave resistance to wind, and protected the roof against projectiles. The roofs of the main tower and other castle buildings were usually surmounted at the ridge by pairs of mythical dolphins called *shachi,* the male occupying one end and the female the other. These figures, made of tile or metal and sometimes gilded, were considered as guardians against evil spirits.

Gables of several types decorated the exterior of the main tower. They included the *chidori-hafu,* resembling a triangle with slightly curving roofs, and the *kara-hafu,* a curved Chinese-style gable also extensively used in the shoin architecture of this period. The number of gables on the outside, however, was not indicative of the number of floors inside, which usually varied between three and seven, with the exception that no towers were built with four floors. The reason for this exception is a superstition: in spoken Japanese the word for four *(shi)* is the same as the word for death.

Chutelike openings called *ishiotoshi*—actually trap doors for dropping stones on the enemy—protected the corners of many of the main towers and other strategic points. Another defensive device consisted of long poles with pails at the ends for pouring boiling water on the attacking forces.

The main towers of the larger castles were often surrounded

by subsidiary towers called *shotenshu.* In some cases these lesser towers were connected to the main towers; in others, they were independent structures. Underground passages were sometimes constructed from the shotenshu to facilitate escape or the starting of counteroffensives.

The nonmilitary structures within the castle compounds were usually in the shoin or the sukiya style of architecture.

■ 2
The Shoin Mansion

■ THE *shinden* style employed for the mansions of court nobles in the Heian period (794–1185) was the first Japanese architectural expression in dwellings of major size. Residences in this style consisted of buildings connected by covered passages which surrounded a garden with a meandering brook. These houses were designed for luxurious living, and the brook was considered a necessity as an ideal place for composing poetry.

It was no wonder that the court nobles, who spent their time in ceremony, in wearing handsome costumes, and in writing poetry, were to lose political power to the military class. As a consequence, in the 13th century a new style of architecture developed to meet the needs of the warrior class. The *buke* style of dwelling which housed the warriors was surrounded by walls with large gates; the galleries of the shinden style disappeared.

Shoin architecture originated in the shinden style and embraced the buke form. The shoin style adopted many of its forms from the Zen sect of Buddhism. The chapel of a Zen monastery differed from that of other sects in that it was a place for living and study rather than for worship. It contained a desk or shoin and a recessed altar usually with a statue of Bodhidharma, the founder of the sect. Often a small window was located above the shoin to provide light. This room came to be called the shoin, and the use of its features gave the name to the new style of architecture: *shoin-zukuri* or shoin style. The altar of the Zen room became a recess in which pictures were hung, and the shoin simply became a platform with a window above it. The series of shelves built into the wall at one time served to store papers and books.

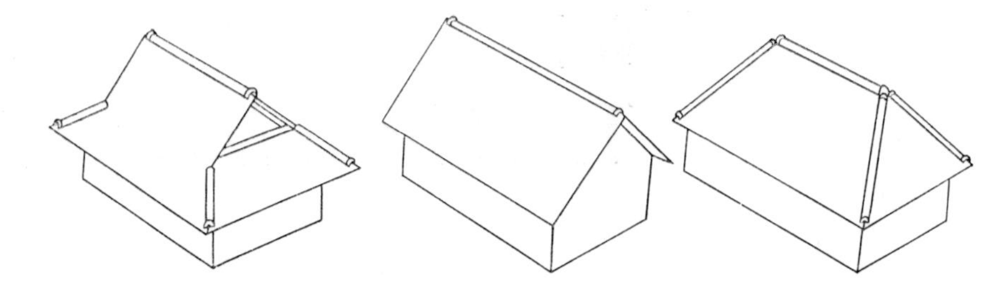

13. Roof Types: Irimoya (left), Kirizuma (center), and Shichu (right).

The shoin style was adopted by the samurai and nobles rather than by the commoners, who built simpler houses. The style developed during the Ashikaga period (1393–1573), reached its height in the Momoyama period, and degenerated at the beginning of the Tokugawa period (1615–1868). Early traces of the shoin style can be seen in the top floors of the Golden Pavilion (Kinkaku) of the Rokuon-ji, originally built in 1397, and the Silver Pavilion (Ginkaku) of the Jisho-ji, which dates from 1488. The former was almost totally destroyed in 1950 in a fire set by an obsessed student monk but has since been restored. The top floors of both buildings have bell-shaped windows, and the Silver Pavilion displays a shelf arrangement similar to that of the shoin.

The plan of a shoin building was rectangular and called for three or more rooms completely surrounded by a corridor or porch. This porch could be open to the outside or enclosed by sliding doors or shutters. When there was more than one large shoin building, the structures were usually connected by covered corridors which joined the buildings at the corners so as not to sacrifice the light at the sides.

The roofs of shoin buildings were constructed of tile or bark. Three types of roof shape were used: the gabled roof or *kirizuma,* the hipped ridge roof or *shichu,* and the hipped and gabled roof or *irimoya.* The gables were usually ornamented with carvings and metal decorations.

The entrance to a shoin building was through a *genkan* or entrance porch of sufficient size for a person being carried in a palanquin to be brought under the shelter of the roof. This entrance porch was also the place where rough footwear for

14. Entrance Porch (Genkan). The genkan was of sufficient size to permit palanquins to discharge their passengers under the shelter of the roof.
Kangaku-in

15. Tokonoma. This type of alcove with a raised base probably developed as a stationary wall on which to hang paintings.
Konchi-in

16. Arrangement of Shelves (Chigaidana). Shelves of differing height form the chigaidana, above which a cabinet with sliding doors is often placed.
Emman-in

17. Window-and-Shelf Alcove (Tsukeshoin). This type of alcove, from which shoin architecture derives its name, originated as a writing desk. *Emman-in*

18. Decorative Doors (Chodaikamae). Doors of this type originally led to an inner closet where bodyguards could be concealed. *Emman-in*

19. Sliding Doors (Fusuma). Sliding doors, which also serve as walls, are an integral part of Japanese architecture.
Hojo of Nanzen-ji

20. Two Types of Shoji: Koshishoji (left) and Akarishoji (right). Sliding doors covered with translucent paper were essential for the lighting of shoin buildings.
Hojo of Nanzen-ji

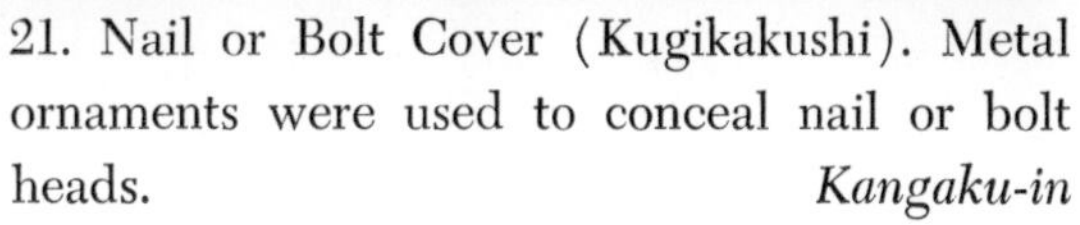

21. Nail or Bolt Cover (Kugikakushi). Metal ornaments were used to conceal nail or bolt heads. *Kangaku-in*

22. Finger Grip for a Sliding Door (Fusuma Hikite). Metal fittings recessed in the fusuma served as finger grips for sliding the doors. *Emman-in*

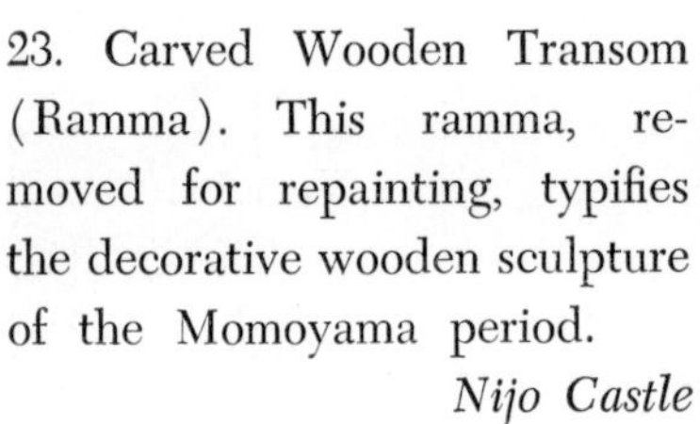

23. Carved Wooden Transom (Ramma). This ramma, removed for repainting, typifies the decorative wooden sculpture of the Momoyama period. *Nijo Castle*

24. Cedar Doors (Sugido). Cedar doors were used as separators in the corridors surrounding shoin-style rooms. *Emman-in*

25. Doors between Porch Sections (Wakishoji). Doors of natural wood served as separators on the outside porches of shoin buildings.
Emman-in

26. Sliding Shutter Doors (Mairado). Mairado, usually paralleled by sliding shoji doors, can be moved to open half the door space or lifted out to open all of it. *Nijo Castle*

27. Shutters (Shitomido). This type of shutter can be raised and fastened to the porch ceiling to let in light and air. *Hojo of Nanzen-ji*

28. Railings (Koran). Koran were designed for decoration rather than protection. The metal newel cap is Chinese in origin. *Sambo-in*

29. Upper and Lower Porches (Hiroen and Ochien). Porches of natural wood break up the area under the roof which protects the inner shoin rooms from the weather. *Hojo of Nanzen-ji*

outdoor use was changed for soft slippers suitable for walking on the tatami mats and polished wooden floors.

In the main room of the shoin-style dwelling, seated upon a small platform called a *jodan,* the master held his audiences. The jodan was located in an elevated section of the room known as the *jodan no ma,* or elevated chamber. Adjoining this section were two or more levels of lower elevation on which the visitors sat according to rank.

The floors of the inner rooms were covered with tatami. These mats, still used in the traditional Japanese house, are approximately three feet by six feet, with slight variations in different localities. They consist of a thick rough matting of rice stalks covered with a thin smooth matting of woven rushes bound with cloth along the lengthwise edges. In the Momoyama period the different colors and designs of the binding indicated the ranks of those allowed to use the rooms. It is a common misconception, however, that the Japanese have always used tatami. It is generally thought that they were introduced in the Muromachi period (1333–1573), but it was not until the end of that period and during the Momoyama period that tatami covered the greater part of the floor space.

The tokonoma or raised alcove is probably the best known form in Japanese architecture. There are many theories regarding its origin, but it is thought to have developed as a stationary wall area on which to attach the popular hanging-scroll paintings (kakemono) that were introduced from China. Prior to this development the walls were all composed of sliding doors, which were not suitable for hanging pictures. In the Momoyama period, pictures were often painted on the rear wall of the tokonoma.

On one side of the tokonoma there is an arrangement called the *chigaidana,* which consists of two or more shelves placed at different levels and connected by vertical supports. No individual shelf covers the entire width of the alcove, but the arrangement is artistically placed and is usually decorated with gold-plated fittings. Above the shelf arrangement there is another shelf enclosed by small sliding doors.

On the opposite side of the tokonoma from the chigaidana is the *tsukeshoin.* The back of this recess juts out into the surrounding corridor and contains a window. In the recess is a raised wooden platform that can be used for writing. The window is often bell-shaped or of wooden grillwork backed with translucent paper.

On the inner side of an elevated room there was usually a decorative arrangement of sliding doors elaborately painted and set in a heavy wooden framework. This, called the *chodaikamae,* originally led to an inner closet which, in the Momoyama period, was used by bodyguards as a place of concealment. The framework of the doors was decorated with metal fittings. Knotted cords with tassels were also affixed.

Fusuma or sliding doors with skillfully executed paintings are representative of the Momoyama period. The decoration of the Momoyama fusuma varied widely from light monochromes to the rich colors and powerful strokes of the Kano masters. The fusuma were often covered with gold leaf, which created a resplendent air and helped in the diffusion of light. Large-size paintings were also necessary to decorate the wide wall areas in the oversize castle structures.

The ceilings in shoin architecture varied widely in ornateness. Double-compartmented, coffered, and tessellated ceilings were common. Often the coffers were painted with birds, flowers, and other designs. Metal fittings decorated the intersections of beams. Plainer boarded and panel ceilings were used over the porches.

Shoji, the light sliding doors used in Japanese houses, are made of translucent paper (popularly called rice paper in the West but actually made from the paper mulberry) pasted on frames of intersecting wooden strips. They are of two types: one with a solid dado and with paper only on the upper half *(koshishoji),* the other completely covered with paper *(akarishoji).* Shoji were especially important in shoin architecture because the surrounding of the rooms with porches cut off considerable light.

Decorative metal fittings on the chodaikamae and the ceiling beams have already been mentioned. Metal fittings were also recessed in the fusuma to serve as finger grips for sliding purposes. They were of various shapes and bore a decorative design or the crest of the owner of the house. There were also metal ornaments called *kugikakushi* which concealed nail or bolt heads.

The *ramma* was a carved wooden transom used to give a feeling of separation of space while allowing free circulation of air. The ramma of the Momoyama period were elaborately carved and brightly painted. In some instances the carvings on one ramma presented different subject matter on each side.

Shoin architecture employed a variety of doors and shutters in addition to those already described. Among these were the *sugido,* doors of cedar adorned with paintings and used as separators within enclosed corridors. The paintings, done against the grainy background of the wood, produced a pleasing decorative effect. Unpainted wooden doors called *wakishoji* were used to separate the sections of open porches. The *shitomido* was a shutter of wooden slats arranged in checkerboard fashion which, when open, was raised and fastened to the ceiling beams of the porch to let in light and air. Another type of shutter, the *mairado,* consisted of wooden sliding doors that ran on tracks parallel to the outer shoji. There were also the *itatobira,* folding wooden doors that opened to the outside through solid walls.

The *hiroen,* a wide covered porch of wood which could be either open or enclosed, was another feature of shoin architecture. The *ochien* was a narrow lower porch that paralleled the outer edge of the hiroen. Porches were often supplied with a *koran,* a low railing usually of two or three horizontal rungs and designed more for decorative purposes than for protection.

■ 3
The Sukiya Teahouse

■ THE ARCHITECTURAL structures so far considered in this book were monumental in scope, for the Momoyama period was one of prosperity, pomp, and grandiose display. However, during this period there developed another type of architecture which was quite the opposite. This style is called sukiya, and the embodiment of sukiya style is to be found in the teahouse or *chashitsu*. The four principles of Sen no Rikyu (1521–91), the greatest tea master of all time, were harmony, reverence, purity, and silence. We may also apply these principles to sukiya architecture.

The sukiya style is light in form, small in size, natural in material, and asymmetrical in plan. The large thick beams, the elaborate carvings, and the glittering paintings of the shoin style are replaced by small, rough, sometimes curved limbs and natural clay and bamboo fixtures. The enormous heavy-tiled roofs are replaced by simple bark or thatched ones.

Nobunaga and Hideyoshi were patrons of the tea ceremony, and there were teahouses in both Azuchi and Fushimi castles among the imposing military structures and those in the shoin style. There were also buildings of the shoin plan built in the sukiya style, and it will be convenient to refer to this style as shoin-sukiya. The only verified example of this style that remains from the Momoyama period is the Hiun-kaku, originally at Jurakudai and now at the Nishi Hongan-ji in Kyoto. While both the shoin and the sukiya styles reached their peak in the Momoyama period, the combination of these styles, the shoin-sukiya, culminated in the fifty years following this era. The best examples are the Rinshun-kaku of the Sankei-en Gardens at Yokohama and the buildings of the Katsura Detached Palace in Kyoto.

The tea ceremony was introduced by the Zen sect of Buddhism from China. Under the patronage of Yoshimasa, the eighth Ashikaga shogun, it became established on a secular basis. At first, the area used for the ceremony was a section of the dwelling house partitioned off by screens. This was called a *kakoi,* and the term is still used for a tea ceremony within a dwelling. Sen no Rikyu is thought to have designed the first independent teahouse.

The independent teahouse and often those connected with a larger building have a roofed bench in the garden as a waiting place *(machiai)* for guests to sit prior to the tea ceremony. From the waiting place a landscaped path *(roji)* leads to the entrance of the teahouse. Carefully arranged steppingstones embedded in earth suggest the way. Before the entrance to the teahouse one finds a stone lantern *(ishidoro)* and a cleansing basin *(tsukubai)* also of stone. A bamboo dipper, used for purification, is laid across the basin of water with the open side down. Often one or more round stones are placed at the foot of the basin so that the overflowing water will not splash when it hits the ground.

Teahouses are classified according to size, the smaller ones of not more than four and a half mats being known as *koma,* while those larger than this go by the name of *hiroma.* Near the door of the koma one notices a rack called a *katanadana.* In former days, this served as a place for male guests to deposit their swords before entering, since the presence of such weapons within would destroy the atmosphere of the tea ceremony. One enters the koma through a *nijiriguchi,* a small square door only a few feet in height. To pass through this low aperture, even those of the highest rank must humble themselves, and the smallness of the door tends to dissociate the participants from the outside world. On the other hand, the entrance to the hiroma, called a *kininguchi,* is of standard size and has sliding shoji.

The orthodox tearoom is about nine feet square or four and a half mats, including a hearth. However, a tearoom can vary from two to nine or more mats in size.

Since the tea ceremony calls for subdued light, the teahouse has shoji windows. The lack of weight in the structure makes it possible to locate small windows at any point, both to produce a decorative effect and to give light to important sections.

30. Covered Outside Waiting Bench (Machiai). Guests arriving for a tea ceremony assemble at the machiai in the teahouse garden.
Zangetsu-tei

31. Stone Lantern (Ishidoro) and Cleansing Basin (Tsukubai). The stone lantern and basin are essential features of the teahouse garden.
Shoko-ken

32. Path with Steppingstones (Roji). Steppingstones lead the way through a simple landscaped garden to the teahouse. *Shoko-ken*

33. Sword Rack (Katanadana). This survival from Momoyama days, when swords were tabu in the tearoom, is suspended from the outside wall of the teahouse.
Shoko-ken

34. Low Entrance (Nijiriguchi). In humbling himself to enter this small door, the tea-ceremony participant dissociates himself from the outside world.
Shoko-ken

35. Entrance to a Large Teahouse (Kininguchi). The entrance to a large teahouse is formed by sliding shoji doors. *Zangetsu-tei*

36. Teahouse Window. The small size of the teahouse makes it possible to have windows anywhere without interfering with structural members. *Shoko-ken*

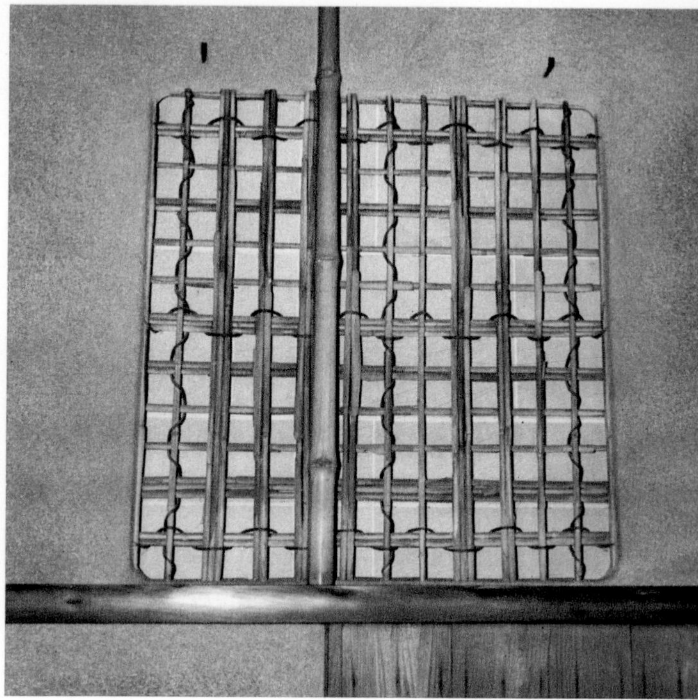

37. Unframed Latticework Window (Shitaji-mado). This unframed window of interwoven bamboo is typical of the teahouse and the natural materials used in its construction. *Fushin-an*

38. Pillar (Nakabashira) and Wall with Open Lower Section (Sode-kabe). This arrangement serves as a partial room divider, concealing the shelf used by the tea master but permitting observation of tea-ceremony movements. *Shoko-ken*

39. Shelves (Tana). The shelves used by the tea master are located behind a wall with an open lower section. A special window provides light. *Shoko-ken*

40. Room for Preparing Tea (Katte no Ma), with Pantry (Mizuya). The katte no ma, adjoining the tearoom, has a pantry for washing, storing, and displaying utensils. *Shoko-ken*

41. Sunken Brazier for Heating Teakettle (Ro). A small square recess in the teahouse floor houses a brazier for heating the kettle in winter. *Shoko-ken*

Typical of the classical teahouse is the *shitajimado,* an unframed window with latticework of interwoven bamboo and reeds. Vertical sections of bamboo with a shoji window make an arrangement similar to that in castle architecture called a *renjimado.*

A tablet with the name of the teahouse appears either on the outside or the interior of the structure, most frequently high on an inside wall. This plaque, usually of grainy wood and bearing the calligraphy of a notable religious figure or some other important person, lends a contrast to the rustic texture of the ceiling.

In winter, the water for tea is heated over a fire in a square container called a *ro,* which is sunk in the floor. In the latter part of the Momoyama period, a new architectural feature appeared in the teahouse: a curved wooden pillar called a *nakabashira* which was connected with the *sodekabe,* a wall whose lower portion was open. There are two opinions regarding the probable reason for this innovation: first, that it served to introduce a curved line among the otherwise straight lines of the structure and, second, that the pillar was essentially a structural form used to support ceilings of differing heights. The open section of the adjoining wall permits the guests to see the preparation of the tea but hides the shelf used by the tea master. The area behind the pillar and its open wall is called the *temaeza.*

The host at a tea ceremony enters through the *sadoguchi,* a different door from that used by the guests. There may also be another entrance, the *kyujiguchi,* which is used by servants bringing in tea. In the latter case, there is usually a *katte no ma,* a room adjoining the tearoom where the tea is prepared. Within this room is a section called the *mizuya,* which serves for the washing, storage, and display of utensils.

Decorative effects are achieved by the use of the simplest materials, such as branches with bark, bamboo, earthen walls, and various reeds. The lower section of the walls is covered with paper of a neutral color, and the sliding doors are of equally inconspicuous design and color. The ceilings are of interwoven rustic materials and differ in each section of the teahouse. Although many materials are considered and much time is spent in designing the effect, the interior should look as though it had no pattern. Similarly, the utmost care is given to selecting the most desirable utensils for the tea ceremony.

Okakura Kakuzo, author of *The Book of Tea,* states: "In the tea-room the fear of repetition is a constant presence. The various objects for the decoration of a room should be so selected that no colour or design shall be repeated. If you have a living flower, a painting of flowers is not allowable. If you are using a round kettle, the water pitcher should be angular. A cup with a black glaze should not be associated with a tea-caddy of black lacquer. In placing a vase or an incense burner on the tokonoma, care should be taken not to put it in the exact centre, lest it divide the space into equal halves. The pillar of the tokonoma should be of a different kind of wood from the other pillars, in order to break any suggestion of monotony in the room."

Sukiya architecture displays a simplicity, a subtlety of taste, and a communion with nature that are typically Japanese. It is noteworthy that Hideyoshi, with his grandiose displays of lavishly decorated architecture, often retreated from castle to teahouse for the simplicity and charm that it offered. The flavor of sukiya architecture can be detected today in any home of merit. It is the essence of good Japanese architecture.

■ 4
Paintings, Gardens, and Gates

■ TO THE Westerner, a chapter about paintings, gardens, and gates might seem out of place in a book about architecture, but in the Momoyama period these three were integral parts of architecture. Paintings furnished the inner decoration within the buildings; gardens were in close harmony with architecture; and gates set the mood for the architecture within.

PAINTINGS

The vigor shown in the new types of architectural construction in the Momoyama period produced new expressions in the field of painting. The large rooms associated with castle architecture required large compositions of sufficient boldness to be seen within the expanses of these areas. The walls, sliding doors, tokonoma, decorative doors, ceilings, and the dadoes of shoji doors were painted with sequential compositions. Gold was often used as a background, for it helped to brighten the dark interiors. Bright colors and bold strokes gave added strength to the paintings. The folding panel screens called *byobu,* which were used to decorate or compartment the rooms, were painted in a similar fashion. Together, these paintings on walls, doors, and screens were known as *shohekiga.* Momoyama screens are considered the finest of those created in Japan, and they comprise a vast and interesting subject. But because most of them are now in museums and private collections all over the world, rather than with the architecture for which they were created, no effort has been made to treat them in detail in this book.

The Momoyama style of shohekiga can be traced from two main currents of painting. The first is the Yamato-e or Japanese style, which is characterized by delicacy, neatness, and the use of bright colors. The other is that employed by the Chinese-style painters of the Muromachi period, which calls for strong monochrome brush strokes. Kano Motonobu (1476–1559) was the first to blend these styles, but his paintings lack the brilliance and size of those created by the Momoyama masters. His grandson, Kano Eitoku, can be said to be the pioneer of Momoyama painting.

Eitoku (1543–90) was commissioned by Nobunaga to paint the shohekiga for Azuchi Castle. Although the castle was destroyed by fire, descriptions of these paintings remain to show that he used both traditional Chinese and Japanese subjects. Some of the works were monochromes, but most of them were of bright colors on a gold background. Eitoku painted only the most significant portions of his subject. This practice was followed by other painters, and in the Nishi Hongan-ji as well as Nijo Castle there are pine trees represented which show neither the base of the trunk nor the top branches.

It should be noted here that Eitoku could not have done all the works ascribed to him. Although he may have been related in some way with most of them, he also had numerous assistants and pupils, as did many of the great painters of Japan. Because of the custom of not signing paintings at this time, there is much doubt concerning the authenticity of many works reputed to be his. It should also be noted that since Eitoku was one of the greatest painters of the Momoyama period, it is natural that owners of paintings in his style should want to attribute them to him.

Kano Sanraku (1559–1635) was such a favorite of Hideyoshi that Hideyoshi asked Eitoku to adopt him into the Kano family. Actually, Sanraku was the son of Kimura Nagamitsu. He is thought to have painted at Jurakudai with Eitoku and Kaiho Yusho. After Eitoku's death, Sanraku and his son Sansetsu (1590–1651) were the representatives of the Kano school in Kyoto, the others having moved to Edo (Tokyo) with the Tokugawa government. Sanraku followed Eitoku's style very closely and painted diverse subjects, mostly in color against gold backgrounds.

Kano Mitsunobu (1565–1608), the elder son of Eitoku, painted in Hideyoshi's camp at Nagoya (Kyushu) in 1592 and later went to Edo to work for Ieyasu. Mitsunobu's younger brother, Takanobu (1572–1618), was appointed official artist at the imperial court—a position previously held by members

42. Detail of Painting by Kano Motonobu, Sounding Waterfall Room.
Hojo of Nanzen-ji

43. Painting on Sliding Doors, Second Waiting Room, Tozamurai.
Nijo Castle

44. Paintings by Kano Tanyu, First Tiger Room. *Hojo of Nanzen-ji*

45. Detail of Metalwork and Door Paintings, Audience Hall, Ohiroma. *Nijo Castle*

of the Tosa school. He was the father of Tanyu, Naonobu, and Yasunobu, who were all important painters of the early Edo period.

Kano Tanyu (1602–74), grandson of Eitoku, was appointed artist of the shogunate when he was sixteen. He painted at Nijo Castle in 1625 and also at Nagoya Castle. His scrolls of the legends of the Toshogu Shrine at Nikko in 1636 illustrated the life of Ieyasu.

Kaiho Yusho (1533–1615), a painter who favored Chinese-style monochromes over the more colorful painting of the period, painted at Jurakudai in 1587 and later for the Katsura Detached Palace. He is noted for the excellence of his brush strokes in monochromes.

Hasegawa Tohaku (1539–1610) tried to break the Kano dominance of the period by reverting to the ink-painting style of Sesshu. His favorite subjects were monkeys, dragons, and tigers. Unkoku Togan (1547–1618) also tried to revive the style of Sesshu. His Chinese landscapes are especially excellent.

The wood carver fulfilled requirements similar to those of the painter. His job was to decorate, and the carvings of the Momoyama period were painted with the same bright colors as the shohekiga. Hidari Jingoro, who is considered to be Japan's greatest wood carver, has been given the dates 1594–1634, but his life seems to be more legend than history. He is known as the originator of many of the carvings from Fushimi Castle, but if the dates assigned to him are correct, he would have been only two years old at the time of its completion. It is possible, however, that he contributed to the decoration of the castle before it was finally demolished. Because he was skillful with his left hand, he acquired the nickname of Hidari, which means left in Japanese. He was considered to be quite eccentric and would only work when he needed money, but his name is linked with the most skillful and ornate carvings of the period.

GARDENS

According to conventional classification, there are three main types of Japanese garden: the landscape garden with a pond and hills; the level garden, which can be symbolic, decorative, or landscaped; and the teahouse garden, which is designed to dissociate the teahouse from the outside world. The gardens most representative of the Momoyama period are those of the landscape type designed to be viewed from the porch of a building. Although paths are suggested in Momoyama gardens, the walk-through garden such as that of Katsura Detached Palace is a slightly later development. The chief component of the Momoyama garden is a large number of rocks, their size corresponding with the size of the structure from which the garden is to be viewed. This harmony between structure and garden is apparent in three gardens which have survived from the Momoyama period in much their original form: those of the Nijo Castle, the Nishi Hongan-ji, and the Sambo-in. These gardens will be discussed later along with the buildings for which they were designed.

GATES

To the uninitiated, a gate might seem to be merely a protective measure, but to the Japanese architect it means a great deal more. The style of a gate sets the mood for the architecture within. If a gate is small and simple, it is probably the entrance to a teahouse or other structure similar in size, but if the gate is large, curved, and ornately decorated, those who enter expect such a theme to be executed within. A gate also dictates one's movement. It is placed so that the guest must enter from the appropriate and most suitable sector. The gate frames the architecture in the day and protects it at night.

■ PART TWO
Representative Examples

■ *BECAUSE both the imperial and military capitals of Momoyama-period Japan were located in or near Kyoto, we find the most important architecture in this area. Fires, earthquakes, storms, and wars have taken their toll of Momoyama architecture, but we are fortunate enough to have many original examples in existence. The largest number of these come from Fushimi Castle, the buildings of which were dismantled and distributed throughout the Kyoto area, mainly to shrines and temples. Other castles were not so fortunate. Azuchi Castle was destroyed by fire three years after its completion; Osaka Castle was destroyed in the sieges of 1614 and 1615; and Nagoya Castle was destroyed by bombing during World War II. Many shoin buildings and teahouses have experienced similar fates.*

The Japanese, with the possible exception of the postwar generation, have always held the history of their country in high esteem. A place or building associated with a historic person or event is highly cherished. Because of this, architecture connected with history is usually revered, kept in good condition, and preserved in its original state. The principle of repairing historically important structures without altering the original form enables us to see Momoyama-period buildings today almost as they were some three and a half centuries ago.

The examples chosen for this book are those which most closely approximate their original condition. All are thought to be authentic except the teahouse Fushin-an at Omote-Senke, which was recently constructed after the design of the original. The datings for the examples in this book are thought to be accurate, although the shoin buildings of Nijo Castle must carry an alternate date of 1625, since there is lack of precise informa-

tion to support fully the author's assumption that they came from the Fushimi Castle of 1596. With these exceptions, all examples are believed to be within the dates of the Momoyama period, 1573–1615. The era is unusual in that the limits of the architectural period do not extend beyond those of the historical period.

A problem connected with the authentication of Momoyama structures is that many of them have been moved one or more times. Each time a building is moved, the paintings on plaster walls (such as the back wall of a tokonoma) must be repainted. The sliding doors are often repainted to match, but then, again, the original may be retained. Also older sliding doors may be installed in new buildings. Thus, dated painting on plaster indicates the last time a building was moved, but not when it was originally constructed.

The examples that follow are grouped according to their primary location so that a general idea of original plans can be considered. Thus the castle structures, shoin buildings, and teahouses which all came from Fushimi Castle will be considered under that title. Three general categories of castles, palaces, and independent structures will be given in that order. The appendix briefly lists other important examples of Momoyama architecture not covered in this book.

Photographs, plans, and elevations most accurately portray the following examples, but supplementary material on history, style, and plan should add to the appreciation of these buildings. In pictures and plans where the scale is not clear, it will be helpful to remember that a tatami mat is about six feet by three feet.

■ 5
Azuchi Castle

■ ODA NOBUNAGA chose a hill on the shores of Lake Biwa, a few miles from Kyoto, to build one of the most advanced castles of his time. This strategic location enabled him to control the principal north-south and east-west routes near Kyoto and to check the power of his three main adversaries. Its proximity to Kyoto also gave him easy access to the imperial court and permitted Nobunaga to take advantage of the titles bestowed by the emperor as recompense for his restoration of buildings at the Imperial Palace.

The promontory known as Azuchiyama rises about 660 feet from the shores of Lake Biwa. The castle placed thereupon was extraordinary in that it introduced many advanced forms never before used in Japanese military architecture. The system of multiple concentric courts and the complexity and ornateness of the seven-story main tower were completely new. It is this fact which makes some historians think that European influences might be responsible. This appears quite possible when one remembers the zeal with which Nobunaga embraced Portuguese customs. He was known to have worn Portuguese clothes; he had a negro servant; and he was in contact with Jesuit missionaries.

The construction of Azuchi Castle was started in 1576 and completed about three and a half years later. Some of the building material was taken from the Nijo Palace (not to be confused with Nijo Castle), which Nobunaga built for the Shogun Ashikaga Yoshiaki. Unfortunately, Azuchi Castle was burned to the ground in 1582 by Mitsuharu, a cousin of Akechi Mitsuhide, the leader of the revolt in which Nobunaga was killed. Nothing but stonework remains. The stone foundation

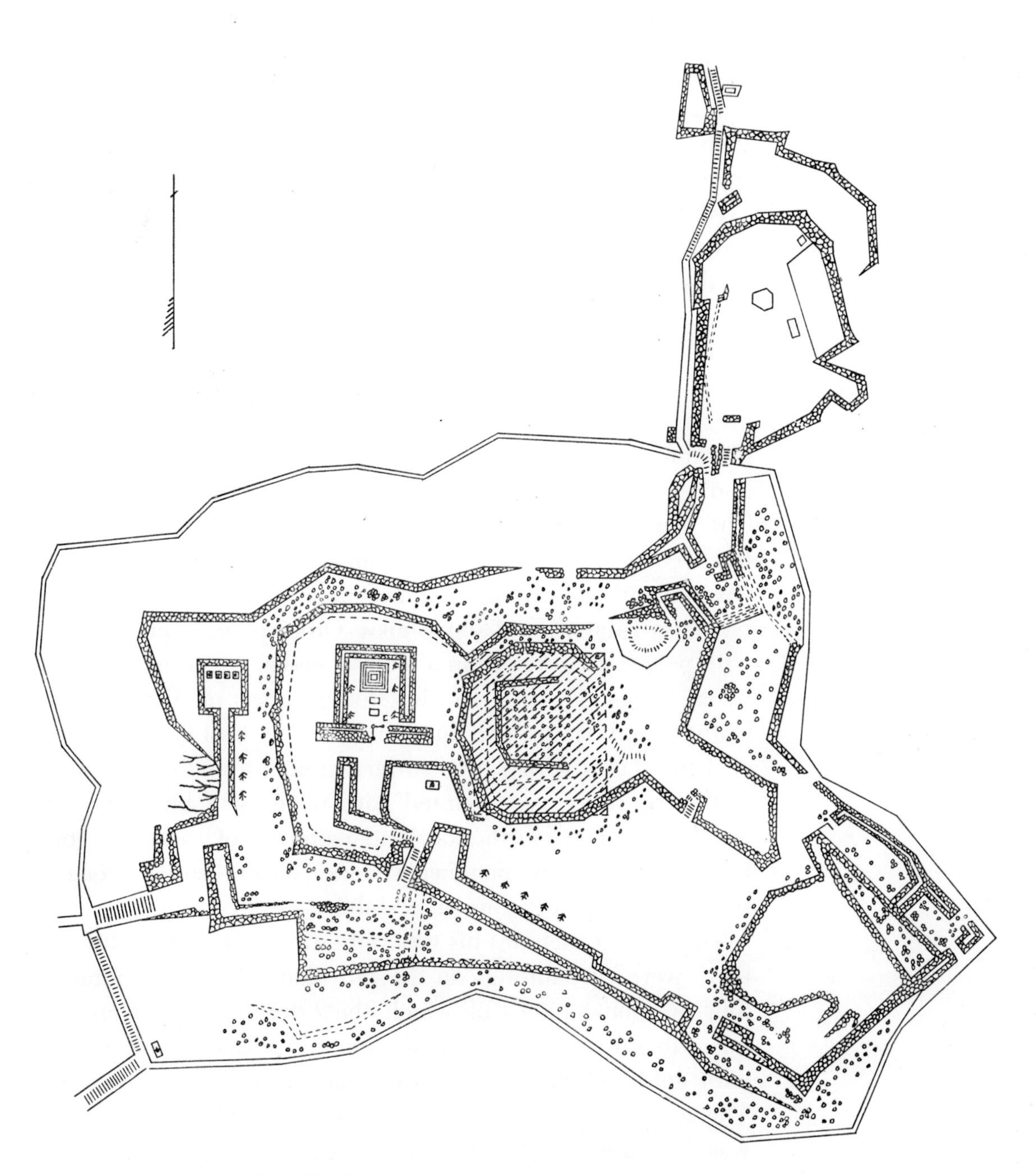

46. Plan. Shaded area represents location of main tower.

of the main tower can still be seen on the summit of the promontory, and from this site the beautiful scenery of Lake Biwa, with the mountains on the far side and the plains on the near, reveals the importance of the location for reconnaissance.

Although no original plans or pictures of the castle buildings have been preserved, we are fortunate in having a description of the main tower by Nobunaga's counselor, Izumi no Kami Toshikazu, in a work called *Nobunagaki.* We learn from this account that the construction of the castle was begun in February 1576 and that laborers, masons, carpenters, tile moulders, artists, smiths, and lacquerers were summoned from the surrounding provinces. The main tower was seven stories high and had sixty openings with black iron doors to provide light. The first floor was contained within the stone foundation. On the second floor there was a room of twelve mats with walls covered with gold from top to bottom and decorated with plum blossoms painted by Kano Eitoku. Other rooms were adorned with paintings of monks in a temple, geese, peasants, and Confucian sages. There were also storage areas on this floor for clothes, food, lamps, and ammunition. The third floor consisted of many rooms with a total surface area of about one hundred mats. The walls were painted with pictures of birds, flowers, and horses. The fourth story had paintings of rocks, dragons, bamboo and tigers, paulownia trees, falcons, and a scene of two people leading cows to a stable.

Toshikazu concludes his description by saying that although there were no paintings on the fifth floor, the sixth contained four octagonal rooms of which the exterior pillars were lacquered with vermilion while the interior pillars were lacquered with gold and decorated with scenes of preaching Buddhas. The seventh or top story was a room of eighteen mats which was decorated inside and out with gold leaf and had dragons painted on the pillars.

From Jesuit records, we have information that after the work had been completed, Father Gnecchi Organtino and other Jesuits went to Azuchi to see the new castle. Nobunaga was so pleased with their visit that he offered them a site for both a house and a church at Azuchi, and the Jesuits accepted.

The town of Azuchi, which was once the military capital of Japan, is now just a country village. There has been talk of rebuilding the main tower of Azuchi Castle, but the money for such a project will have to come from outside the quiet village, since Azuchi's population consists mainly of people who live off the land and the fish of Lake Biwa.

■ 6
Osaka Castle

■ OSAKA Castle was the largest and most heavily fortified castle ever built in Japan, yet we know very little about its original form. The castle in its entirety survived for only about thirty years. Nothing but the stonework of the main compound remains from the original, although some of the towers and the tenshukaku have been restored. Outwardly, the main tower may have some resemblance to the original, but this structure, which was restored in 1931, is made of reinforced concrete and has an elevator to the top.

Before Hideyoshi's castle was constructed, the site was occupied by a branch temple of the Hongan-ji sect built in 1496. The temple was besieged in the 16th century by Nobunaga during his crusades against the temple fortresses and was laid in ruin. Osaka was a strategic location, and after Nobunaga's death Hideyoshi planned to build a castle there. Actually, he wanted to move the capital to Osaka, but the emperor and the principal monasteries refused to move.

We are fortunate in having a description of the construction of Osaka Castle by the Jesuit Padre Frois, as recorded by James Murdoch in *A History of Japan:* "The walls are of great amplitude and height—all of stone. In order that the multitude of workers should not cause confusion, it was ordained that each master should have his determined place, where he should work, a great number of people being employed during the night in emptying the water which continually kept rising in the fosses. What is the cause of much marvel in this matter is to see whence such a great number of stones of all kinds of sizes have been taken; there being a great lack of them there. For this reason he commanded the

47. Southwest Corner, Main Tower.

48. West Side of Main Tower.

49. Corner Tower on Inner Moat.

50. North Side of Main Tower.

51. Rampart across Outer Moat.

52. Wall Construction of Main Compound.

53. Stonework on Inner Side of Moat Walls.

54. Outer Entrance of Measuring Gate.

neighbouring lords for twenty or thirty leagues around to send boats loaded with them. In this way the city of Sakai alone has been charged to dispatch 200 vessels every day. So that from our house we sometimes saw as many as 1,000 entering under full sail and in good order together. On discharging, the stones are placed with such care and heed that none (without leaving his head there) might take a single one of them to place it elsewhere. And in order that the work might go forward with greater heat, it happening that a lord who supervised fell short either in men or industry, he was at once sent into exile, and stripped of his States and revenues. Besides the towers and the bulwarks around the fortresses, which are visible from afar by reason of their height, and the splendour of the tiles, which are all gilded, he is rearing many other remarkable edifices there."

Construction of the castle began in 1583, when 30,000 men were put to work on it day and night. The number of workers was later doubled, and the castle was completed in three years. Strategically, the site was well chosen. To the east flowed the Yamato River and to the north the Yodo, while the western approach was protected by the *yokobori* (flanking moat) and the southern by the *karabori* (empty moat). The circumference of the castle area, which contained a central compound and its surrounding second and third compounds, was approximately eight miles. To the north of the main compound was an enclosure, the Yamasato-maru, in which was located the Kita no Mandokoro, the compound designed for Hideyoshi's wife. The castle itself had no fewer than 48 large towers and 76 smaller ones. The chief of these, a structure of some eight stories, stood on a stone base 75 feet high and rose above this to a height of 102 feet. It was topped with a roof of gilded tiles and ornamented in characteristic style with a pair of gold dolphins. Cranes and tigers, respectively symbolizing long life and prowess, decorated the exterior walls of the top floor.

At the present site, which comprises the foundations of the innermost citadel, several massive blocks of stone can be seen. The largest of these, known as the Tako Stone and used in the Sakura "measuring gate," has a front section 26 feet high and more than 36 feet long. Two other large blocks of comparable size remain. Near the main tower is the well called Kimmeisui (gold-sparkling water), whose reportedly inexhaustible supply of water was a boon to the Toyotomi family during the sieges of 1614 and 1615.

Osaka was the seat of the military government from the time of the completion of Osaka Castle until Hideyoshi moved to Fushimi Castle in 1596. After his death in 1598, Hideyori, his son, and Yodogimi, the mother of Hideyori, moved to Osaka Castle. It was not until 1614 that Tokugawa Ieyasu was able to question the position of Hideyori. Using as a pretext an allegedly unfavorable inscription that Hideyori had caused to be carved on a bell at the Hoko-ji in Kyoto, Ieyasu attacked Osaka Castle with a force of 150,000 men. The effort to take the castle was futile, however, for it was nearly impregnable. A peace treaty was drawn up with the provisions that Hideyori would retain permanent control of the castle and the land he owned and that the garrison of the castle would not be punished. In compensation for the effort made by the Tokugawa forces, it was agreed that they be allowed to demolish a portion of the castle's defenses. Ieyasu lost no time in ordering several thousand men to start tearing down walls and filling in moats. Too late, the Toyotomi forces discovered that more than the agreed number of moats had been filled in. Ieyasu again attacked the castle, this time with about a third of the previous number of troops, and through trickery prevented Hideyori from counterattacking. Hideyori was forced to commit suicide; his mother was killed by a retainer; and thirty others took their own lives when the castle fell.

The castle, which was greatly damaged in the siege, was restored by the Tokugawa government in 1660, but in September 1868 the buildings were destroyed by fire. The present main tower, which was constructed in 1931, is a five-gabled structure of ferroconcrete over a steel frame and rises to a height of 135 feet above its 45-foot stone foundation. Its design was taken largely from a contemporary screen painting. The interior, which has seven floors serviced by two elevators, is a museum containing relics of Hideyoshi and the original castle. During World War II, troops were stationed in the castle, and further damage resulted from bombing. Some of the canals in the present industrial city of Osaka were once the outer moats of the castle.

■ 7
Fushimi Castle

■ AT THE height of his career, Toyotomi Hideyoshi built the most magnificent fortified collection of structures ever assembled in Japan. This castle-palace has given its name to the era in Japanese history called the Momoyama period. There is, however, a good deal of confusion over the name of the castle, since it is frequently referred to as Momoyama Castle, Fushimi Castle, or Fushimi-Momoyama Castle. It was located in Fushimi, a town which is now a southern suburb of Kyoto. About one hundred years after its destruction peach trees were planted upon the hill where it once stood; hence the name Momoyama, or Peach Hill. Because of its many lavish buildings, it is also called a palace, but the extensive fortifications justify the use of the word castle. I prefer the name Fushimi Castle, since the term Momoyama was not known during its existence, and this term avoids confusion with the name of the period.

Fushimi was important strategically because it was on the direct road between Osaka and Kyoto. There is a plain between Osaka Castle and Fushimi Castle, and it was said that a fire signal in the tower of one could be seen from the tower of the other. This was possible topographically, although the distance was twenty-five miles. I know of Fushimi people who said they watched the fires from the World War II bombing of Osaka from the site of Fushimi Castle.

Fushimi protected the capital city of Kyoto from the south, the only side not bounded by mountains. Hideyoshi was able to make river navigation possible from the Inland Sea to Fushimi Castle via the Yodo River and the Uji River, which he dredged and diverted. A lesser man than Hideyoshi might not have chosen this site, since the Emperor Kammu, the founder of Kyoto, was buried near there. Whether Hideyoshi moved the grave is not known. In 1912, the Emperor Meiji was buried on the site of the castle, and this has made it very difficult to explore the old location, since most of the area is considered sacred.

There seem to have been three major reasons why Hideyoshi built Fushimi Castle. First, he had given his Kyoto palace, Jurakudai, to his adopted son Hidetsugu, and when his own son Hideyori was born, Hideyoshi planned to give Osaka Castle to the latter. This would have left Hideyoshi without a residence. A second reason was that he needed a sufficiently impressive residence for the reception of a mission from China, which country he planned eventually to subjugate. A third purpose for the construction of Fushimi Castle was to reduce the wealth of the daimyo in northeastern Japan. The southwestern daimyo had been severely taxed to finance and supply the expedition to Korea, and it was part of Hideyoshi's plan to tax the other daimyo in men and money for this new project and thereby to make sure that they were not becoming too powerful financially.

Hideyoshi had had much experience in building castles. Before Fushimi, his most famous fortresses were of the type built on a plain (hirajo), such as those of Osaka and Nagoya. Fushimi was to be a castle of the plain-and-mountain type (hirasanjo) like those of Hikone and Wakayama.

It is thought that work on Fushimi Castle was started in 1594 and completed in 1596, but some records suggest that work may have begun as early as 1592. The *Taikoki,* a biography of Hideyoshi, states that 250,000 men were at work on the castle in 1594, but this number seems large, even for such grand projects as his.

The main road to Fushimi, known as the Fushimi Kaido, was constructed, and the road leading to the castle site was broadened. Daimyo were ordered to contribute men and material. Huge blocks of stone were secured from Daigozan and Untanzaka, and timbers from the Kiso district were floated down the rivers. The quota of men to be supplied by each daimyo for labor service was determined on the basis of his income, which was measured in terms of the rice harvested from his estates. The rate was 300 men per 10,000 *koku* (approximately 49,629 bushels). Hideyoshi made out a sectional

55. Fushimi Castle as Recreated in a Painting by Ota Tenyo (1884–1943).

work schedule for each of the daimyo, who were required to build certain sections within a specified time. He supervised the construction himself, and this probably greatly accelerated the completion of the work. In one of his letters concerning the undertaking, Hideyoshi stressed the importance of "taking good care of the catfish"—an allusion to the ancient Japanese belief that a huge catfish living at the center of the earth caused earthquakes by moving its tail when it was angered.

In 1595, having become convinced of the disloyalty of his adopted son Hidetsugu, Hideyoshi forced him to commit suicide. Then, in his great distaste at the whole affair, he ordered the dismantling of the Kyoto palace of Jurakudai, which Hidetsugu had occupied. A few of the buildings considered suitable for Fushimi Castle were reconstructed there. The Hiun-kaku is thought to have been moved at the same time.

Fushimi Castle was completed in 1596. Hideyoshi summoned villagers from Nakamura of Owari (where he was born) to come and live in Fushimi, promising them land and building materials. He similarly advised residents of Osaka, Sakai, Amagasaki, and Kyoto to migrate to Fushimi. Perhaps as an antidote to homesickness, the names of the streets in Fushimi were copied from those of places where the settlers originally lived. At the turn of the century, Fushimi was a large town, comparable in size to Kyoto, Osaka, and Sakai and larger than Edo (now Tokyo). Since the best artisans flocked to Fushimi to work on the buildings, it soon became the art capital of the country. Even after the castle was demolished, the town flourished for many years because of the river transportation made possible by Hideyoshi. Fushimi is now part of the city of Kyoto.

Shortly after the castle was completed, lavish preparations were made for the visit of the Ming mission from China. Hideyoshi had planned an *umazoroe* (cavalry exercise) for the reception of the ambassadors. His idea was to have mounted warriors in armor line both sides of the road from Yawata (about seven miles to the south) to the main entrance of Fushimi. For this project, he gathered warriors from the daimyo of the northeastern provinces at the rate of 100 men per 10,000 koku of rice. Each daimyo was assigned a station for his men and their horses. Tokugawa Ieyasu was required to provide 5,000 men, who were stationed at Kusatsu, Ishiyama, Otsu, and Sakamoto. The people of Fushimi and Kyoto, quite naturally,

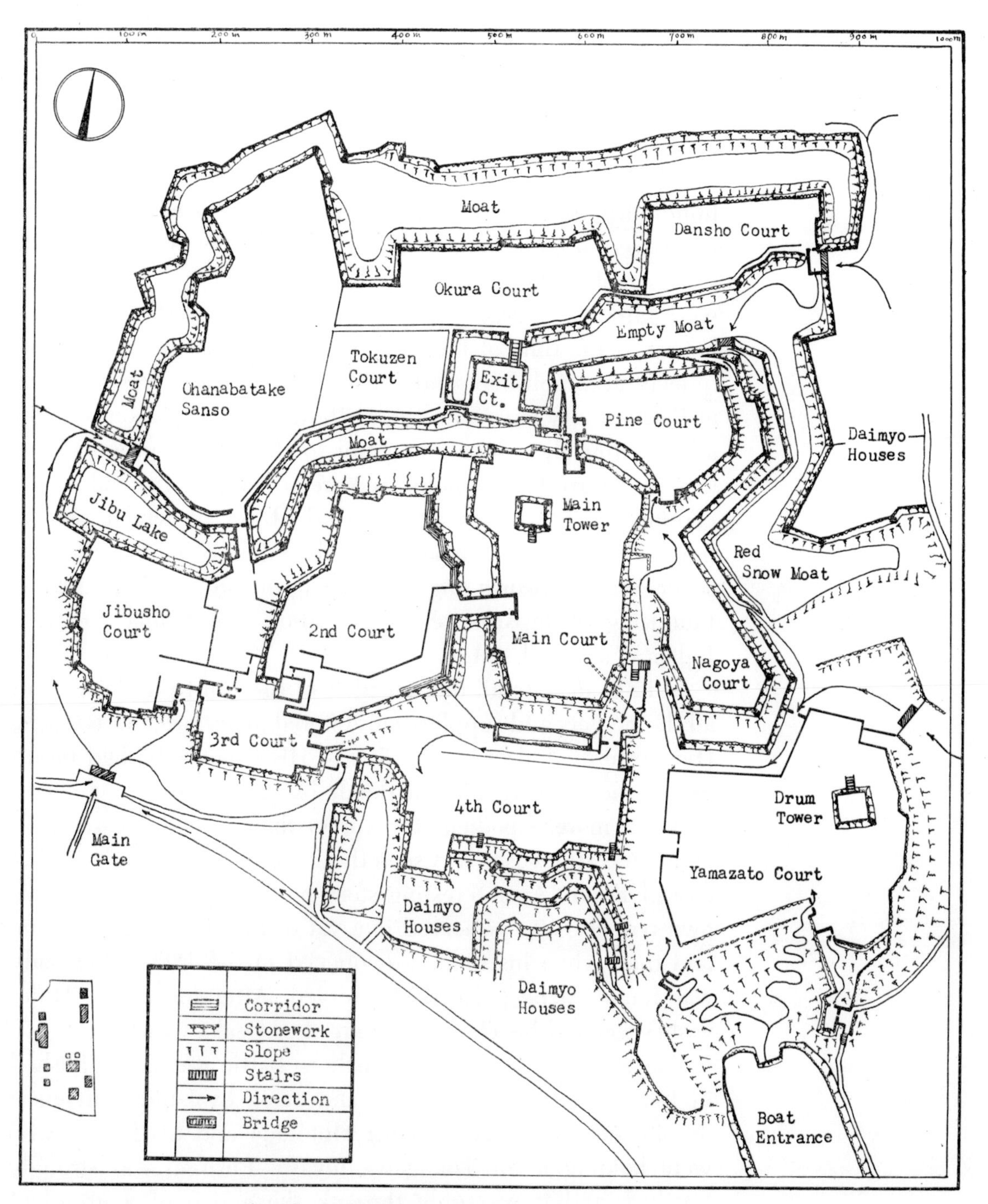

56. Plan of Fushimi Castle by Jiro Kato.

were eager to watch the preliminary drill. Then, three days before it was to take place, the region was shaken by severe earthquakes.

Many buildings in Kyoto and Fushimi were destroyed, and the death toll ran as high as 2,000, including some five or six hundred persons who died within the castle itself. Among the latter were a large number of servants for whom replacements were hastily brought from Osaka. Hideyoshi and his warlords were safe, however, for they were living in one-story thatched houses at the time of the calamity. Repairs on the castle were quickly accomplished, and the Chinese mission was received at Fushimi fifty days after the earthquake. The mission brought a reply from the Chinese emperor to Hideyoshi's proposals for a peace treaty to conclude his Korean venture. Instead of accepting his conditions, the general object of which was to humiliate Korea and make Japan the equal of China, the emperor, to Hideyoshi's anger and chagrin, proposed to appoint him King of Japan—a clear indication that China regarded Japan as a vassal state.

In 1598, despite all the remedies of the court physicians and all the prayers and supplications offered at shrines and temples, Hideyoshi died after a brief illness. His wives, who had promised to accompany him in death by taking their own lives, found it more expedient to express their grief in mere wails and tears. Hideyoshi was secretly entombed in the hills to the east of Kyoto. An interesting story has it that his body, at his own request, was preserved in a vat of the strongest rice wine and that, when his tomb was opened in the 1880's, the body was found to be perfectly preserved. After his death, Hideyoshi's son and his chief wife moved to Osaka Castle.

The initiation of Fushimi Castle to battle was accomplished in 1600, when it was attacked and taken by Ishida Mitsunari despite the resistance of Torii Mototada and his forces, who were holding it for Tokugawa Ieyasu. Fushimi was strongly fortified, and it was only through the action of a group of traitors who fired the castle from within that Ishida's forces were able to seize it. The defenders, who according to some reports comprised 2,000 men, refused to surrender, although they were greatly outnumbered. After most of them had been killed, Mototada assembled the survivors (tradition says there were 384 of them), and the entire group committed suicide.

Fushimi Castle continued to be a place of considerable importance until 1615, when the Toyotomi family was exterminated. Tokugawa Ieyasu took some of the structures for Nijo Castle, which was constructed in 1603. From that time on, buildings from the castle were given to temples as the Tokugawa saw fit. The final demolition of Fushimi was probably started in 1620, after the death of Ieyasu, and it is known that some of the stonework was used to repair Yodo Castle in 1623. Iemitsu, the grandson of Ieyasu, enlarged Nijo Castle in 1625 and added some of the remaining structures.

The main tower was supposedly moved from Fushimi to Nijo in 1625. But because it is also reported to have been burned in the attack of 1600, it is doubtful that the original was moved. It seems more likely that a reconstructed tower was taken from Fushimi to Nijo. This tower was probably not as large or as lavishly decorated as the original. In any event, the tower that was moved to Nijo was struck by lightning in 1791 and destroyed.

Fortunately, many of the gates and other structures from Fushimi Castle still exist today. They are mostly in the possession of shrines and temples in the Kyoto and Lake Biwa areas. None of these establishments, however, are located in the heart of Kyoto, which has been repeatedly plagued by fires, but remain on the fringe of the city.

At the site, very little can be seen of the original castle. The northern moat and the lake called Jibu-ike retain their original shape but are lacking stonework. Mounds remain with a few rocks where the main tower and the drum tower were located, but this area is closed to the public. The tomb of the Emperor Meiji occupies the south end of the section which was once the main compound.

Work is now under way to rebuild the main tower. Unfortunately, it will not be located where the original once stood. I have seen the model of the proposed structure and must regretfully report that in my opinion the project is a commercial venture rather than an effort to reproduce historically accurate architecture.

Besides the examples from Fushimi Castle that follow, three rooms from the castle attached to the Hojo of Nanzen-ji will be treated with that building in Section 10. The appendix contains a list of other structures from Fushimi Castle.

57. View from Front.

The Gate of the Sambo-in at Daigo

The Sambo-in gate is representative of the less ornate style of the early part of the Momoyama period. It is a *hirakaramon* or flat Chinese gate, which has curved gables at the ends, as opposed to the later gates, which had large curved Chinese gables in the front and rear. The size of the gate indicates that it served as the entrance to a fairly small building, probably of the shoin style. The doors are adorned with large *kiri* (paulownia) and chrysanthemum crests. Although the roof is considered as flat, the four corners curve slightly upward. Records do not indicate the year that this gate was transferred from Fushimi Castle to neighboring Daigo, and some are of the opinion that it was originally built in Daigo especially for the cherry blossom viewing party that Hideyoshi held there in 1598.

58. View from Inside.

59. Detail on Inner Side.

60. Carvings under Front Gable.

61. Carvings under Gable at West End.

The Gate at Nijo Castle

The Nijo Castle gate, originally at Fushimi, is a fine example of the *karamon* (usually translated "Chinese gate") style. The word *kara* is the Japanese reading for the Chinese dynasty name T'ang and was commonly used as a general term to designate foreign derivation. In this case it refers to the type of gate with curved gable at front and rear. And in fact, the kara-hafu style of gable so widely used in the Momoyama period owes its origin to China. The roof of the Nijo gate is of *hinoki* (cypress), and the whole structure is decorated with carvings and metalwork. Early in the 17th century the paulownia crest of Hideyoshi was replaced by the hollyhock leaves of Tokugawa Ieyasu, and these in turn gave way to the sixteen-petaled chrysanthemum when the castle was taken over by the Imperial Household at the beginning of the Meiji period. The outer panels of the gate are ornamented with carved cranes, flowers, and butterflies and the inner ones with *karashishi* (Chinese lions), a tiger, and a dragon. In contrast with other gates in which the lower portions of the gables are connected, the Nijo gate has its side gables open at the bottom. The gate is supported by six wooden pillars, of which the two inner ones are round and the four outer ones square.

62. South View.

63. Detail of East Supporting Pillar.

64. West View.

The Gate at Toyotomi Jinja

The karamon now at the Toyotomi Shrine was transferred first from Fushimi Castle to the Konchi-in of Nanzen-ji and then, in 1876, was moved to its present location at the sanctuary honoring Hideyoshi. The roof of this gate is of cypress and is supported by six wooden pillars. The relief carvings on the doors are especially interesting, although they are simpler than those on other existing karamon of this period. The two exceptionally fine cranes under the front gable are attributed to Hidari Jingoro. The lower extremities of the side gables of the roof are connected.

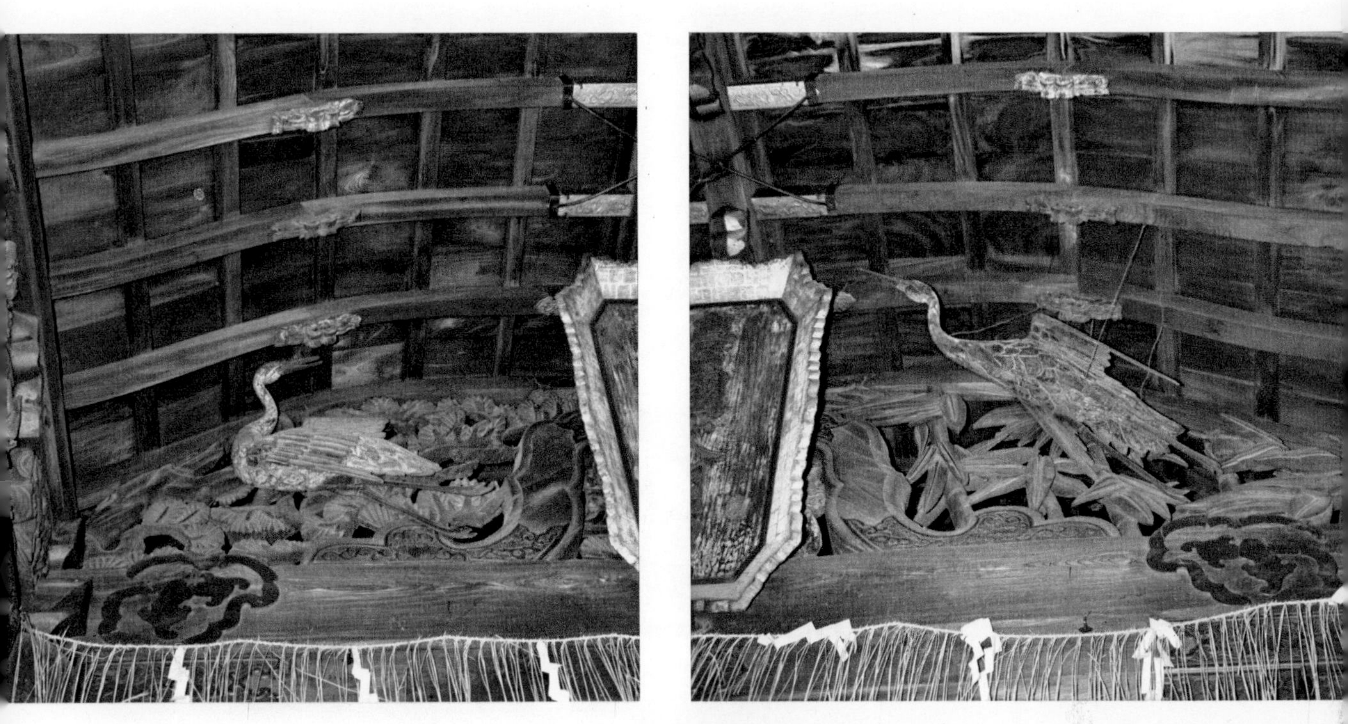

65 & 66. Carvings under Front Gable (North and South Sides).

67. Detail of Door.

68. View of East Side.

69. Underside of South C

The Gate at Nishi Hongan-ji

The karamon at the Nishi Hongan-ji is formally called the Chokushimon (Gate of the Imperial Messenger) but is popularly known as the Higurashi no Mon or "day-spending gate" because the viewer might well spend a whole day in appreciating its beauties. Elaborate carvings cover the entire structure—among them many flowers and animals both real and imaginary. The frolicking karashishi on the doors are particularly well executed. One panel on the inner side portrays Hsü-yu, a legendary Chinese hero and saint noted for his purity. He is pictured beside a waterfall, washing from his ear an offensive proposal from the Emperor Yao. The companion panel on the other side shows a farmer watering his ox and expressing anger at the pollution of the stream. The cypress roof of the gate is supported by six wooden pillars, but because the four outer pillars are the most prominent, the structure is often called a four-legged gate. The inner pillars are round and the flanking ones square. This gate was removed from Fushimi Castle and reconstructed at the Nishi Hongan-ji in 1632.

70. View from Southeast.

71. Carvings and Bracketing.

72. North Side of Door Panels.

73. Detail of Door and Pillar.

74. Northwest Panel.

75. Northeast Panel.

76. View from North.

The Gate at Goko no Miya

This gate of the *yakuimon* type is the only structure from Fushimi Castle remaining in the Fushimi area. It is now located at a shrine in the Momoyama section of Fushimi about a half mile west of where the castle once stood. This type of gate was used for defensive rather than decorative purposes, a fact which accounts for its sturdiness and simplicity. The curved roof is tiled and is topped by tile dolphins. The main rectangular supporting pillars, on a plane with the doors, are backed up by four square pillars to the rear. The roof is not symmetrical, the front area being shorter than the rear. The upper beams are square in cross section. A few carvings ornament the simple bracketing system and the oversized decorative braces under the gables at each end. The lintel is heavy and extends outward to the sides, where it is protected by metal. The area of the doors taken together forms a square. The doors are hung on upturned pins, and there is a small door adjacent to the large one on the west side.

77. Large Bracket and Lintel.

78. West Gable.

79. Detail of South Side.

80. View from Southwest.

The Gate at Kodai-ji

This gate of the yakuimon type is similar to the one at Fushimi. The joints, bracketing, and carvings on the Kodai-ji gate are more complicated and ornate. The ridge of the Kodai-ji gate is not topped by dolphins, but the number and the size of the supporting posts are similar. Carvings on the central section of the lintel represent two dragons under a bridge. Above the lintel in this portion is a curved section which blocks off the ceiling of the gate from the front. The ends of the rectangular lintel extend to the sides, where they are protected by wooden coverings. Together the large doors are square in shape. Small doors are found on both sides of the large ones.

81. Brackets on South Side.

82. Detail of Supporting Post and Lintel Carvings.

83. Base of Supporting Post and Small Door to South.

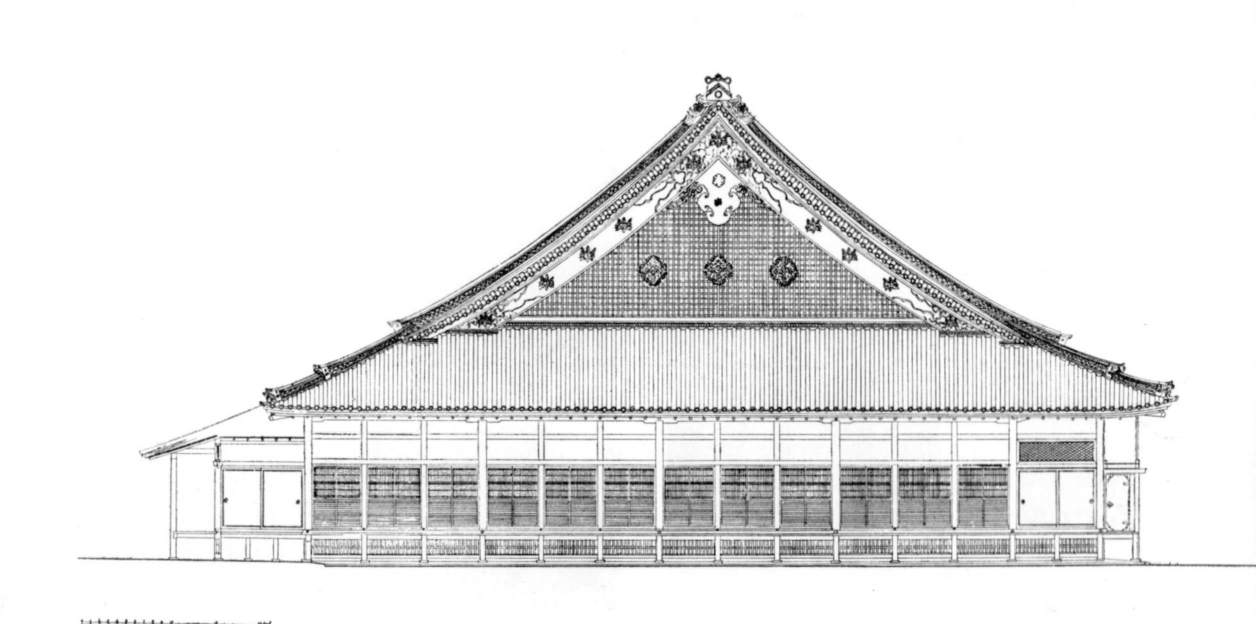

84. South Elevation of Audience Hall.

The Shoin Buildings at Nishi Hongan-ji

A large entrance hall with three rooms, Hideyoshi's Audience Hall (Taimenjo) with its garden, several rooms called the Shiroshoin, and a Noh stage were brought from Fushimi Castle to the Nishi Hongan-ji in 1632. Although many of the interior paintings date from the time when the buildings were reassembled, or perhaps later, the size of the structures and the lavishness of the decorations reflect the glory of the Momoyama period.

The buildings can be entered from the south through the large entrance hall, which has a cypress roof with the traditional Chinese curved gable. The first room is the Nami no Ma or Wave Room, in which both the ceiling panels and the sliding doors are decorated with paintings of waves. To the north of this is the Old Tiger Room, so named for the Kano Eitoku paintings of tigers on its wooden doors. The "old" serves to distinguish Eitoku's tigers from those in paintings of a later date found elsewhere in the Nishi Hongan-ji. The "old" tiger paintings, however, have lost their brilliance and now can hardly be seen. Between the Wave Room and the Old Tiger Room is the Taiko no Ma or Drum Room, which takes its name from the paintings of drums that adorn its ceiling panels. This small room has a tokonoma. Although the gold paper covering

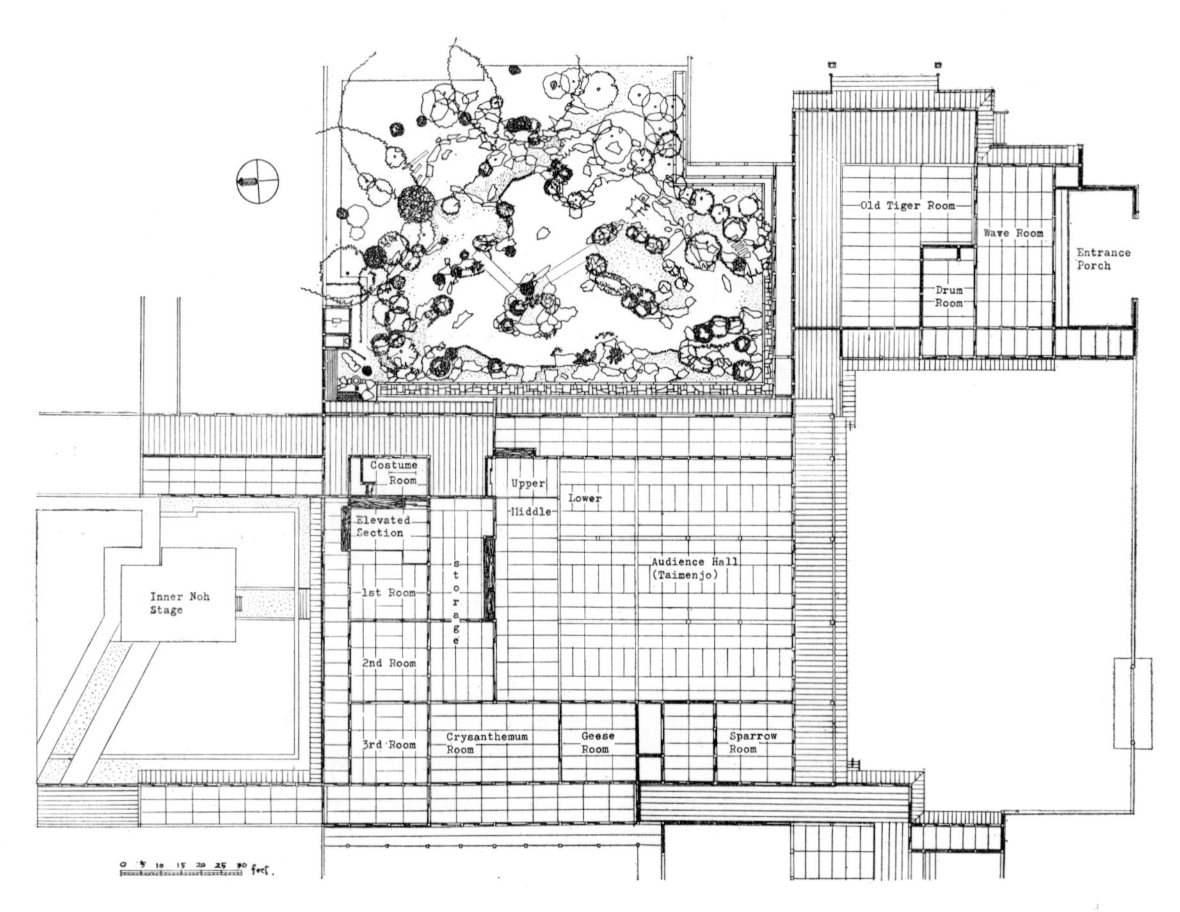

85. Plan of Shoin Buildings.

both the tokonoma and the walls is of a later date, the drum paintings on the ceiling remain in their original state. The room was supposedly used by Hideyoshi when he inspected the heads of slain enemies, and tradition has it that the red in the ceiling was painted with blood. A transom with carvings of grapes and squirrels separates the Drum Room from the Wave Room.

To the south of this large building is a long porch from which one enters Hideyoshi's Audience Hall. The latter structure, usually called the Taimenjo, is also variously referred to as the Oshoin, the Ohiroma, or the Ko no Ma. It is floored with 243 mats, supported by 45 pillars, and divided into three sections of differing levels. The two rows of pillars running north and south divide the lower portion of the hall into three lengthwise sections, and these are further delineated by plaster panels between the pillars near the ceiling and wooden strips between them at floor level which separate the tatami into groups. The pillars are closer together at the north end—an arrangement that makes the room appear longer. At the north or upper end of the hall is an elevated section separated near the ceiling by a transom of flying storks attributed to Hidari Jingoro. It was in this section that Hideyoshi sat during his audiences. The rear wall contains a decorative arrangement of doors and a tokonoma with a large mural painting. On the east is a section of still higher elevation which contains a tsukeshoin and an arrangement of shelves.

All the paintings on the north wall of the middle section are the work of Kano Tanyu. The central one pictures Chang Liang presenting the four sages to the heir apparent of the Emperor Kao Ti, founder of the Han dynasty, while those on the decorative arrangement of doors compose a scene showing an interview of the Emperor Wu Ti of the Han dynasty with the legendary Hsi Wang-mu, "Queen Mother of the West." The paintings in the lowest section are all by Kano Ryokei. The walls and sliding doors are decorated with pine and plum trees, cranes, and other birds; the ceilings display geometric designs, birds, and flowers. A fan-shaped window permits a view of the upper section from the south. For its transom, the tsukeshoin section of this room has a gilded wood carving of a paulownia tree. The coffered ceiling above it is ornamented with paintings of dragons against a gold background.

To the east of the Audience Hall is a long corridor which can be opened to give a view of the garden. Its ceiling is decorated with paintings of books, and its wisteria frieze is the work of Kaiho Yusetsu.

The garden, designed by Asagiri Shimanosuke, goes by the name of Kokei or Tiger Glen, since it is intended to give the impression of a wild mountain valley through which tigers roam. These lordly animals fascinated the Japanese, who had never seen them in actuality until they were encountered in Korea by Hideyoshi's expeditions. Tiger skins were brought back to Japan, and the tiger, with his fierceness and size, inspired the Japanese imagination.

The area of the garden is 95 by 65 feet. In the center is a dry lake of white sand "fed" by a large dry waterfall. It is not unusual, of course, to find such waterless features in a Japanese garden. Two islands representative of the crane and the tortoise (both symbols of long life) are linked with the shore by large curved bridges of stone. As in all castle gardens of the time, many huge rocks of unusual shapes, colors, and surfaces are incorporated into the design. Another interesting feature of this garden is its sago palm trees, a species introduced from Java by the Portuguese. Since the trees are not native to Japan, they must be covered with straw in winter to protect them from the cold. The sago palm was a favorite of Hideyoshi and Ieyasu and can be seen in many of the paintings associated with the two.

West of the Audience Hall are the Sparrow Room (Suzume no Ma), the Wild Goose Room (Gan no Ma), and the Chrysanthemum Room (Kiku no Ma). The first of these derives its name from the paintings of bamboo and sparrows by Maruyama Okyo with which it is adorned. Similarly, the second is named for its paintings of wild geese by Kano Ryokei. The walls and sliding doors of the third display paintings of chrysanthemums by Kaiho Yusetsu, and the ceiling is decorated with a design of fans.

The work of Kaiho Yusetsu also appears in the frieze and the ceiling paintings of autumn flowers in the north corridor of the building. The tsukeshoin of the First Room *(see Figure 105)* juts out into this corridor. On the east side are the doors which Kato Kiyomasa, one of Hideyoshi's generals, is said to have brought from Korea. At the end of the north corridor is the Shozoku no Ma or Costume Room, which has a tokonoma, an arrangement of shelves, and a bell-shaped window. The walls are decorated with a hunting scene by Kaiho Yusetsu.

To the west are three rooms which are thought to have been Hideyoshi's apartment of state. The First Room, also called Shimei no Ma, was apparently the private room of Hideyoshi. It comprises two levels, the upper of which has a tsukeshoin, a tokonoma, an arrangement of shelves, and ornamental doors. Carved transoms and sliding doors separate the three rooms of the apartment. The paintings in the First and Second rooms are the work of Kano Koi and Kano Tanyu. Those of the Third, picturing cherry trees and peacocks, are by Kaiho Yusetsu.

In the court to the north of the large building containing the Audience Hall stands the Noh stage brought from Fushimi Castle. This covered structure does not display the ornate decorations characteristic of the Momoyama period; in keeping with Noh tradition, it was kept simple in order that the audience might not be distracted from the performance itself.

86. Detail of Ceiling, Drum Room.

87. Detail of Painted Door, Old Tiger Room.

88. Detail of Sliding Doors, Wave Room.

89. Porch to South of Audience Hall.

90. Audience Hall, View to North.

91. Middle and Upper Sections of Audience Hall.

92. Northwest Corner of Middle Section, Audience Hall.

93. Upper Section of Audience Hall.

94. Audience Hall, View to Northeast.

95. Mural by Kano Tanyu, North Wall of Middle Section, Audience Hall.

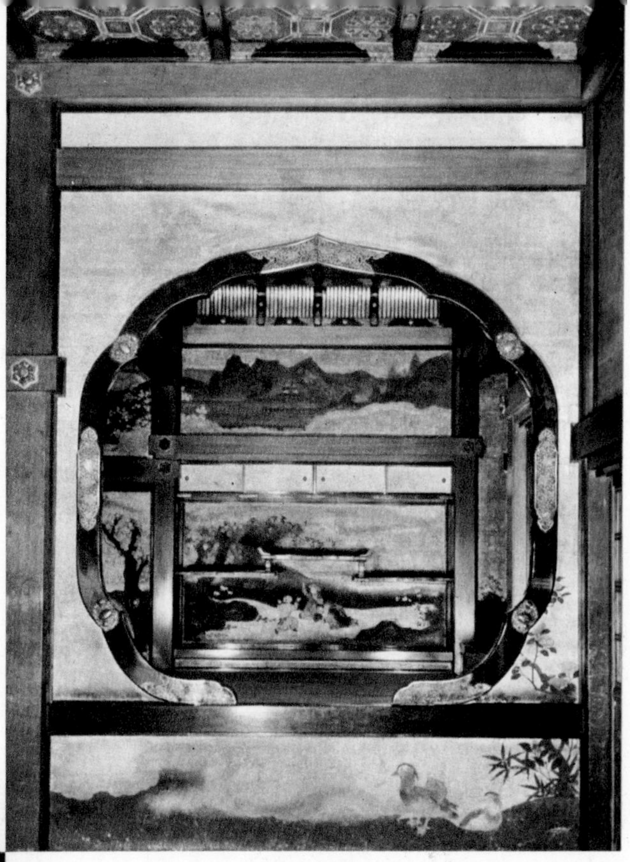

96. View through Fan-shaped Window, Upper Section of Audience Hall.

97. Outside View of Tsukeshoin, Audience Hall.

98. East Corridor of Audience Hall.

99. East Side of Audience Hall and Its Garden.

100. Sparrow Room.

101. Chrysanthemum Room.

102. North Corridor.

103. Costume Room.

104. Korean Doors, North Corridor.

105. Outside View of Tsukeshoin, North Corridor.

106. First Room, Hideyoshi's Apartment of State.

107. Sliding Doors and Transoms of First Room, Hideyoshi's Apartment of State.

108. Sliding Doors and Transoms of Second Room, Hideyoshi's Apartment of State.

109. Third Room, Hideyoshi's Apartment of State.

110. Sliding Doors and Transoms of Third Room, Hideyoshi's Apartment of State.

111. Second Room, Hideyoshi's Apartment of State.

112. Noh Stage.

113. Tozamurai, Shikidai, and Ohiroma.

The Tozamurai, Shikidai, and Ohiroma at Nijo Castle

The five connected buildings in the second compound of Nijo Castle are the best existing examples reflecting the grandiose display of the Momoyama period. Architectural historians have been unable to find documentary proof as to the exact date of these buildings, but it is the author's opinion that the first three are from the Ohanabatake of Fushimi Castle and were transferred to Nijo Castle in 1625, and that the fourth and fifth were constructed at this or a later date. However, because of lack of information, the alternate date of 1625 must be given to all five of these buildings as the year of their original construction.

The first three buildings are covered by tile roofs of the

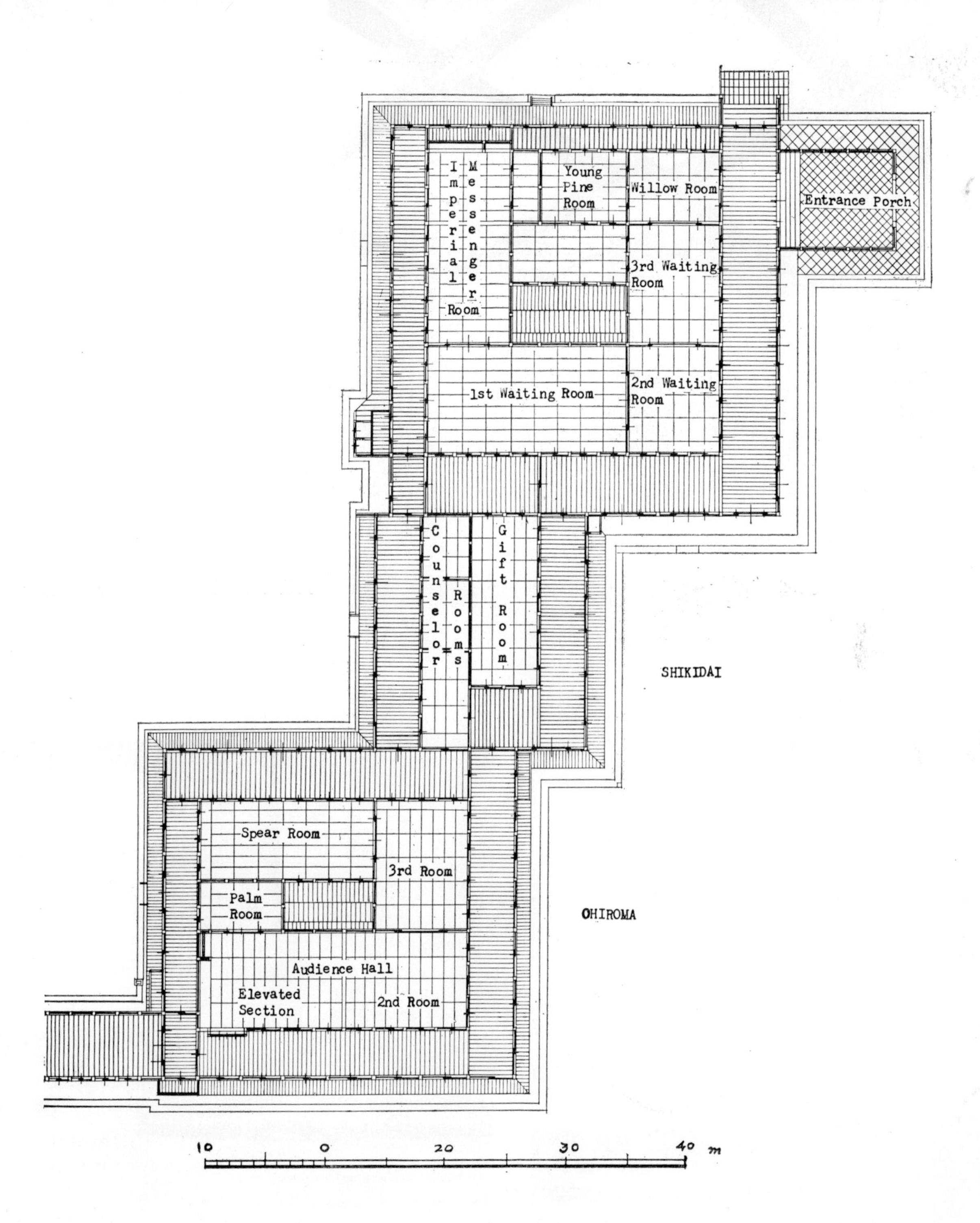

114. Plan of Tozamurai, Shikidai, and Ohiroma.

115. Detail of Corridor Ceiling.

116. Metal Bolt Covers.

117. Decorative Metalwork, Ohiroma.

118. Detail of First Waiting Room, Tozamurai.

119. View of Young Pine Room from Willow Room, Tozamurai.

120. View of Imperial Messenger Room from First Waiting Room, Tozamurai.

121. Arrangement of Decorative Doors, Imperial Messenger Room, Tozamurai.

122. Tokonoma and Chigaidana, East Corner of Imperial Messenger Room, Tozamurai.

123. Corridor between Toza murai and Shikidai.

124. Detail of Cedar Doors in Corridor.

125. Detail of Mural, Shikidai.

126. Mural, Middle Counselor Room, Shikidai.

127. Mural, Spear Room, Ohiroma.

128. Carved Transom, Third Room, Ohiroma.

129. Mural and Transom, Third Room, Ohiroma.

130. Arrangement of Decorative Doors, Audience Hall, Ohiroma.

131. Chigaidana, Audience Hall, Ohiroma.

132. Corridor to South of Audience Hall.

133. Ohiroma and Garden.

134. South Gable, Ohiroma.

135. Detail of Garden.

irimoya style. They connect with each other at the corner sections. The first building, the Tozamurai, is approached through an entrance porch topped by a large Chinese gable. This entrance porch does not retain many of its original decorations except for three large carved transoms.

Each of the buildings is almost square in shape and contains rooms in the central portion surrounded by corridors enclosed by sliding wooden and shoji doors. The floor of the enclosed corridors is called the "nightingale floor" because it was designed to squeak when walked upon, thus protecting the inhabitants from any surprise intrusion. This was accomplished by placing beveled splines under the floor boards. Ramma and colorfully painted ceilings decorate these corridors. Shining plated fittings are used on the woodwork throughout the buildings. The rooms are brightened by paintings of the Kano school. Among these, however, the only ones definitely identified are those of the Shikidai by Kano Tanyu.

From the entrance of the Tozamurai can be seen the Willow Room and the Young Pine Room, which are named after the decorative paintings on their walls and sliding doors. The remainder of the building contains the Imperial Messenger Room and three waiting rooms decorated with paintings of tigers and bamboos against a gold background. Highly colored ceilings add to the richness of the décor, and carved transoms separate the upper portions of these waiting rooms. The most important room in this building, however, is the Chokushi no Ma or Imperial Messenger Room, in which envoys from the emperor were received. It has an elevated section with a tokonoma, an arrangement of shelves, and decorative doors. The paintings in the Chokushi no Ma depict maple trees in autumn.

Sections of the corridors between the buildings are separated by sliding cedar doors adorned with paintings. The second building of the group, the Shikidai, is named for its principal room, in which presents to the shogun were received. One wall of this room is decorated with a mural of two pine trees against a background of gold. Beyond the room are three small chambers once used by counselors of the shogun. Two of these display paintings of ducks, while the third has a painting of herons perched on a snow-covered willow tree.

The third building, the Ohiroma, contains the Audience Hall with its Second and Third rooms, its Yari no Ma (Spear Room), and its Sotetsu no Ma (Sago Palm Room). The Spear Room is distinguished by an imposing painting that occupies both walls and sliding doors and depicts a large hawk perched upon a sprawling pine tree. Between this room and the Third Room is the celebrated peacock-and-peony transom ascribed to Hidari Jingoro—a masterly carving that shows peacocks on one side and peonies on the other. The painting which gave its name to the Sago Palm Room has been destroyed.

The Audience Hall itself, with its many paintings of pines, bamboos, birds, and rocks—all executed on backgrounds of gold—presents a dazzling sight. The elevated north end contains a tsukeshoin, a chigaidana, and ornamental doors. It was in this section of the hall that Yoshinobu, the fifteenth Tokugawa shogun, proclaimed the restoration of administrative powers to the throne in 1868. South of the Audience Hall is an enclosed corridor decorated on the outer side near the ceiling with carvings against a background of shoji.

The garden adjacent to the Ohiroma is attributed to Kobori Enshu. Most prominent of its features are the many large angular rocks—noted for their color in the rain—whose massive forms harmonize with the huge shoin-style buildings and the solidity of the castle structures. It is thought that originally the lake was dry and the garden contained no trees. The present lake, however, is filled with water and has two islands representing the crane and the tortoise.

The Kyakuden of the Konchi-in at Nanzen-ji

This building has been kept in fine condition and is a good example of the middle-sized shoin structure of the Momoyama period. The cypress roof is in the irimoya (hipped and gabled) style. The plan of the structure is rectangular and consists of six rooms, one of which is now used as an altar. The northwest room contains an elevated section with a tokonoma decorated with a painting of a pine tree. A tsukeshoin juts out into the corridor to the west, and to the east of the tokonoma one finds a chigaidana and decorative doors. The First Room contains a raised section; this room can be opened on the Second Room

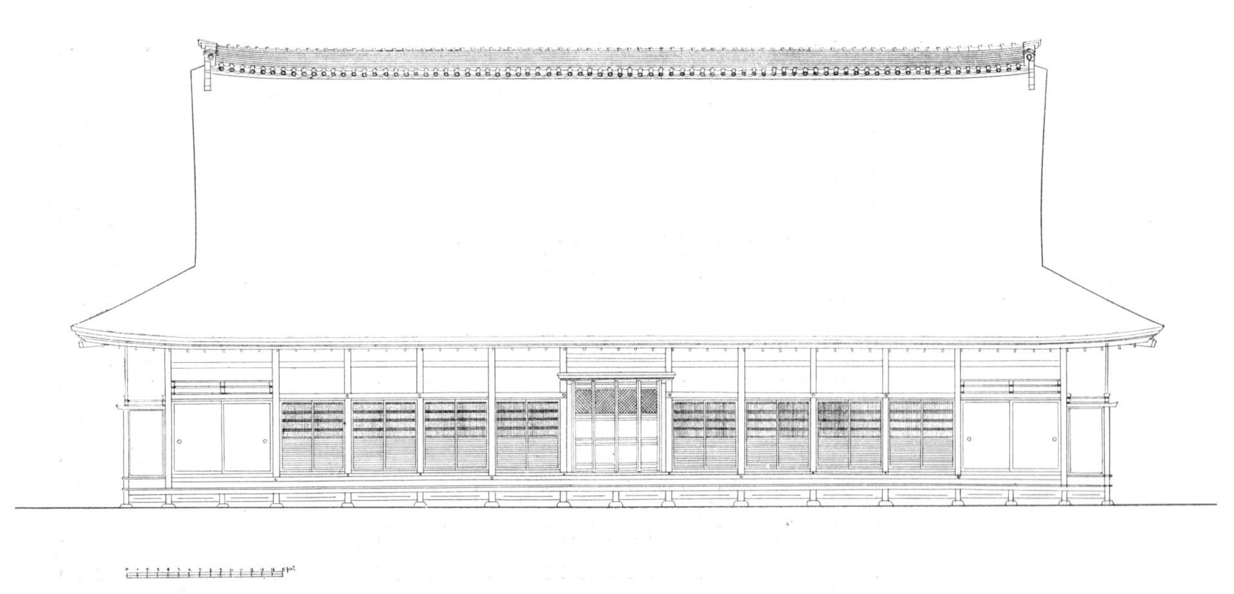

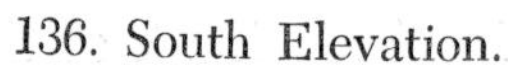

136. South Elevation.

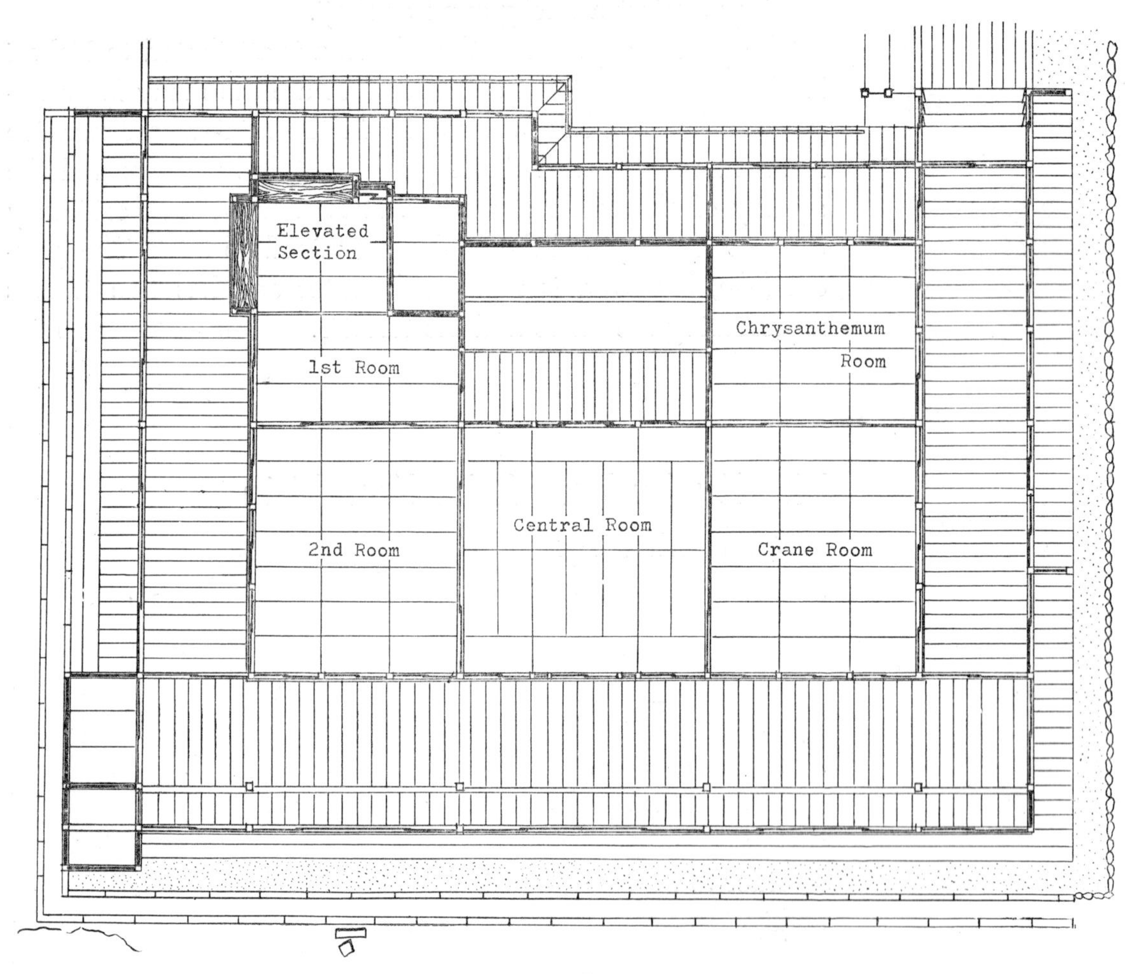

137. Plan.

138. South View.

to the south. Both rooms are ornamented with paintings of pine trees by Kano Naonobu. The rooms of the Kyakuden are surrounded by an enclosed corridor which opens on a garden to the south. Excellent paintings of cranes and of Chinese sages, also by Naonobu, decorate the central room to the south. In the southeast corner is the Tsuru no Ma (Crane Room), with its sliding doors painted by Kano Tanyu and, to the north, the Kiku no Ma (Chrysanthemum Room), with decorations by the same artist.

139. View of Garden from South Corridor.

140. Chigaidana, Northwest Room.

141. Decorative Doors, Northwest Room.

142. Detail of Ceiling, Northwest Room.

143. Detail of Ceiling and Beams of Enclosed Porch.

144. Painting on Cedar Doors.

145. Door Paintings by Kano Tanyu, Crane Room.

146. Door Paintings by Kano Naonobu, Central Room.

147. Door Paintings by Kano Naonobu, Central Room.

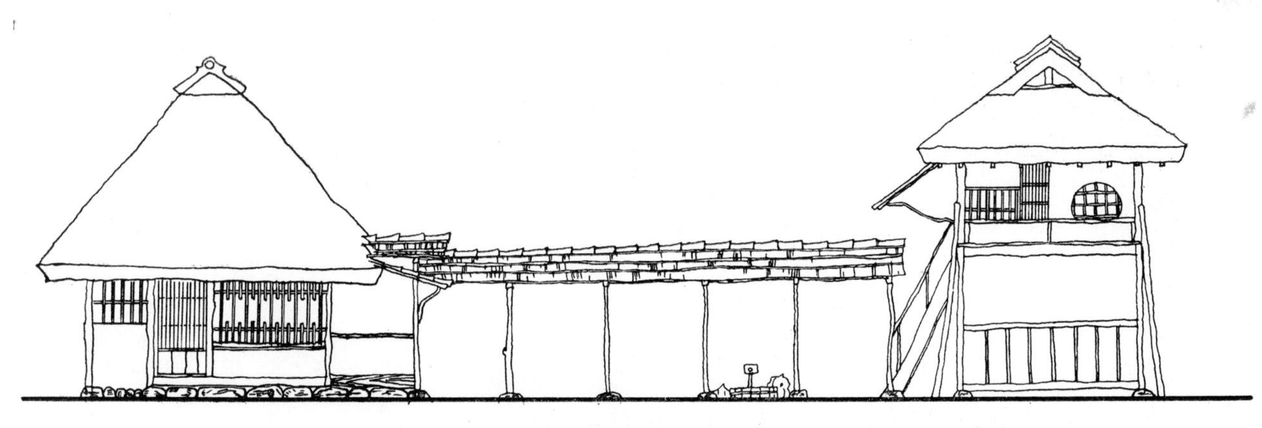

148. West Elevation (Karakasa-tei left, Shigure-tei right).

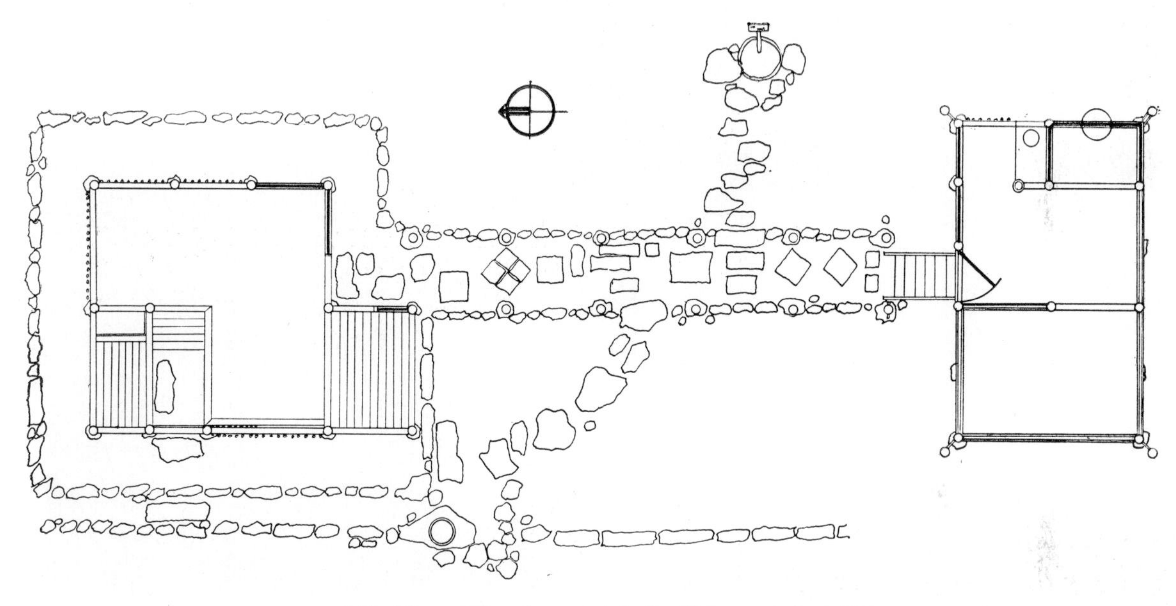

149. Plan (Karakasa-tei left, Shigure-tei right).

The Karakasa-tei and Shigure-tei at Kodai-ji

These two connected teahouses were removed from Fushimi Castle to the Kodai-ji in the early part of the Tokugawa period. They are unique in that they were constructed before the uniform plan of the teahouse became established. Because they were experimental, it is hard to compare them with the other more standard teahouses of the period. The houses are con-

150. Karakasa-tei.

151. Ceiling, Karakasa-tei.

152. West Entrance, Karakasa-tei.

153. Receptacle for Heating Tea, Karakasa-tei.

154. Shigure-tei.

155. Ceiling, Shigure-tei.

156. Upper Section Railing, Shigure-tei.

157. Tokonoma, Shigure-tei.

nected by a walkway protected by a thatched roof. At present, these structures are in very poor condition and are not in usable shape.

The northern building, the Karakasa-tei, has a high-pitched thatched roof that resembles an umbrella *(kasa)* and is supported by bamboo poles and a central wooden beam. The main entrance is on the west side, and the steps from ground level to floor level are within the building. The southwest corner contains a receptacle for heating tea.

The southern building, the Shigure-tei, is two stories in height and is covered by a thatched roof of the irimoya type. The roof is supported by bamboo and wooden beams. The lower story, with an earthen floor, serves as a waiting room, while the second floor contains two sections of differing heights. The upper section has shutters which can be opened on three sides. There is a tokonoma in the lower section with a round window set in the rear. A wall with an open lower section adjoining the tokonoma is of bamboo, as is also the pillar of the tokonoma. Behind this open wall is a receptacle for heating tea.

The Shunso-ro at Sankei-en

This teahouse was designed by Oda Urakusai, a younger brother of Nobunaga and a pupil of Sen no Rikyu. Although it was originally at Fushimi Castle, it is now located in Yokohama and is attached to the western end of a building of later date. The shingled roof is in kirizuma (hipped ridge) style.

The three-and-a-half-mat tearoom is entered from outside through a low door on the south side. To the south is a recessed area one-half mat in size; a wall with an open lower section separates a portion of this area from the rest of the room. A tokonoma containing a shoji window is located to the north. On the east side there are doors for servants and for the host. These doors lead to the above-noted building of later date, which contains a place for washing and storing tea utensils.

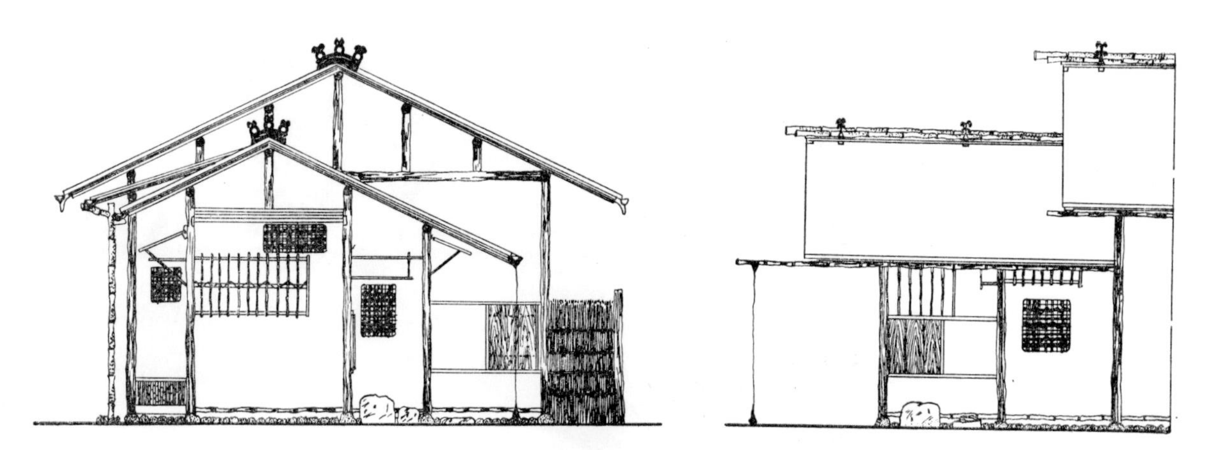

158. West and South Elevations.

159. Plan.

160. West View.

161. Cleansing Basin and Stone Lantern.

162. Low Entrance and Sword Rack.

163. Low Entrance and Windows.

164. Recessed Area to South.

165. Host's Entrance.

166. Tokonoma.

■ 8
Nijo Castle

■ AFTER 1600, when Tokugawa Ieyasu gained partial control of the country by defeating Mitsunari at Sekigahara, he established himself at Edo (Tokyo). In 1602, Ieyasu ordered the construction of a fortified residence in Kyoto to use for his visits to the capital. This structure, called Nijo Castle, was completed in 1603 or 1604 and was located in the west central part of Kyoto. History records that Hideyoshi's son, Hideyori, paid a visit to the castle in 1611, three years before Ieyasu turned against him. In 1625 and 1626, Tokugawa Iemitsu enlarged and repaired the castle, and it was at this time that the main tower and other structures from Fushimi Castle were added. Upon the completion of these repairs, a visit by the emperor was arranged—much on the order of that which took place at Jurakudai in 1588 *(see page 160)*. The lavish entertainment included music, dancing, and poetry parties, and gifts were presented to the emperor and other ranking guests. After 1634, the last year that Iemitsu used the castle, many of the buildings were given away. In 1791, the main tower was struck by lightning and completely destroyed. After the Meiji Restoration of 1868, Nijo became imperial property. In 1871, it was made the prefectural office of Kyoto. Much damage was done at this time, and it was not until 1885 that it was again taken over by the Imperial Household Department. It was given to Kyoto City in 1939.

The original castle constructed by Tokugawa Ieyasu is the one which falls within the Momoyama period. Its plan consisted of one compound, rectangular in shape, with the long sides on the north and south. The main gate on the east side is probably the only original building to survive, and it has been repaired several times. This gate is of the watariyagura (tower gate)

167. Main Gate.

type. The tiled roof is in the irimoya style and is topped by tile dolphins. The gate, supported by large stones, is reached by an earthen rampart across the moat. Its large, heavy doors and the surrounding wooden beams are protected by metalwork. Two small doors are located on either side of the larger ones.

The original main tower of the castle is thought to have been situated near the northeast corner. Unfortunately, very little is known about the details of the castle until after the enlargement and repairs made by Iemitsu. In 1625 and 1626, the west section was considerably extended, and an inner compound surrounded by a moat was added. The northern gate, of the tower-gate type, and the southeast corner tower have been reconstructed as closely as possible to the originals of Iemitsu's time. The difference in the workmanship of the stone walls built by Ieyasu and Iemitsu can still be clearly seen. The main tower from Fushimi Castle was added by Iemitsu, and its stone base still exists at the southwest corner of the inner moat.

168. Main Gate.

169. Main Gate Viewed from Inside.

170. View to West through Main Gate.

171. Detail of Beams, Main Gate.

172. Metalwork on Small Door to North, Main Gate.

173. Southeast Corner Tower.

174. South End of Main Gate.

175. Inner Moat and Base of Tower from Fushimi Castle.

176. Detail of Stonework. Section to right is from original castle; that to left dates from about twenty-two years later, when castle was repaired.

■ 9
Nagoya Castle

■ IN 1610, Tokugawa Ieyasu ordered the construction of a large castle in Nagoya to strengthen his position in central Japan. At this time Hideyori, Hideyoshi's son, was still in power at Osaka Castle, and there were formidable warlords in the western provinces. When the castle was completed, Ieyasu placed his son in charge of it, and it was held by members of the Tokugawa family until the Meiji Restoration of 1868. The castle was almost completely destroyed in an air raid on May 14, 1945. The reconstruction of the main tower and its subsidiary tower was completed in 1959. The new towers, made of concrete, resemble those of the original on the outside, but the inside, which is now equipped with elevators, is of new design. The southwest corner tower of the main compound remains much in its original form.

The original castle was of the type located on a plain and contained main, second, and third compounds plus those known as the Fukai Compound and the West Compound. A palatial group of shoin buildings similar to those of Nijo Castle was located in the main compound. Residences were located in the second compound. The perimeter of the castle was protected by a moat, as was the main compound.

Kato Kiyomasa, one of Hideyoshi's generals in the Korean campaigns, was in charge of building the castle. Kiyomasa was an expert in stone-wall construction, having learned much in Korea to supplement the Japanese knowledge of this subject. He built a high steep base for the main tower and had the construction of the base concealed by large screens on a bamboo framework so that spies could not find out the secrets of his trade. In later reconstruction efforts, it was discovered that he had used within the base a platform of timbers which dis-

177. Original Main Tower (destroyed in World War II).

178. Southwest Corner Tower.

179. Southwest Corner Tower.

tributed the weight of the building above without pushing the walls of the base outward.

The exterior of the original main tower showed five floors, and a sixth was contained within the base. The tower was known for the large number of gables that decorated all of its sides. A covered passageway led to the subsidiary tower. The area of the floor of the main tower immediately above the base was 120 feet by 105 feet, and the top floor measured 55 feet by 40 feet.

The ridge of the new main tower is topped by two gold dolphins whose predecessors had a most interesting history, chiefly because of their great value. Legend has it that a robber named Kakinoki once tied himself to a huge kite and managed to pluck off a few precious gold scales. In 1873, one of the dolphins was loaned for an exhibition in Vienna and, on its return trip to Japan, went down to the depths of the sea when the ship that was carrying it sank off the Izu Peninsula. The dolphin was recovered after six months, but it perished with its mate during World War II. New dolphins of gold, made at tremendous cost at the Osaka mint, were escorted into the city of Nagoya in 1959 by the mayor, brass bands, and flag-waving citizens to take their place on the roof of the reconstructed castle. Each dolphin of the pair (one male and one female) is of copper covered with 560 scales of 18-carat gold and equipped with fins of the same metal—at a cost of $78,000. The reconstruction project was undertaken by the city of Nagoya, which owed much of its early growth to its having been chosen as the site for Ieyasu's castle.

■ 10
Imperial Palaces

■ IT IS known that during the Momoyama period the Imperial Palace was rebuilt by each of the three military rulers, but details on these buildings are few and contradictory.

Oda Nobunaga erected a palace for the emperor in 1571, but no descriptions of this palace have survived. Previous to this time the imperial family had been in dire straits because of civil strife, and Nobunaga's palace, although probably not very large, was obviously an improvement.

In 1592, Hideyoshi erected a larger Imperial Palace. Considering Hideyoshi's record of building on a grandiose scale and his respect for the emperor, this palace must have been much larger and finer than the one provided by Nobunaga. A gate now at Daitoku-ji and a building at Nanzen-ji are the only structures that remain from this palace. The Shishin-den of the Imperial Palace was moved to Ninna-ji, but was destroyed in a fire in 1887.

Ieyasu also rebuilt the Imperial Palace. The references to the buildings are limited and inconsistent, and it is not known when this palace was completed or why it needed rebuilding so soon. It is probable that Ieyasu did not want a palace built by Hideyoshi as the emperor's residence. It is also possible that the palace suffered in the earthquake of 1596, but there are no records indicating this. There are no existing buildings from this palace.

180. Southeast Side.

The Gate at Daitoku-ji

The Chokushimon or Imperial Messenger Gate from the Imperial Palace constructed by order of Hideyoshi was transferred to Daitoku-ji in 1640 as a gift from the Empress Meisho. It is of the karamon type with large curved gables on the front and rear. The roof is of cypress bark and is supported by two central posts plus two round pillars on each side. The carvings on the front and rear panels are of birds; those on the sides, of pine branches. The carvings are comparatively simple for this period, but the bracketing system is complex, reflecting the Chinese style in which imperial palaces were constructed. There is a plaster portion beneath the open gables on the sides.

181. Underside of South Gable.

182. Lintel and Bracketing.

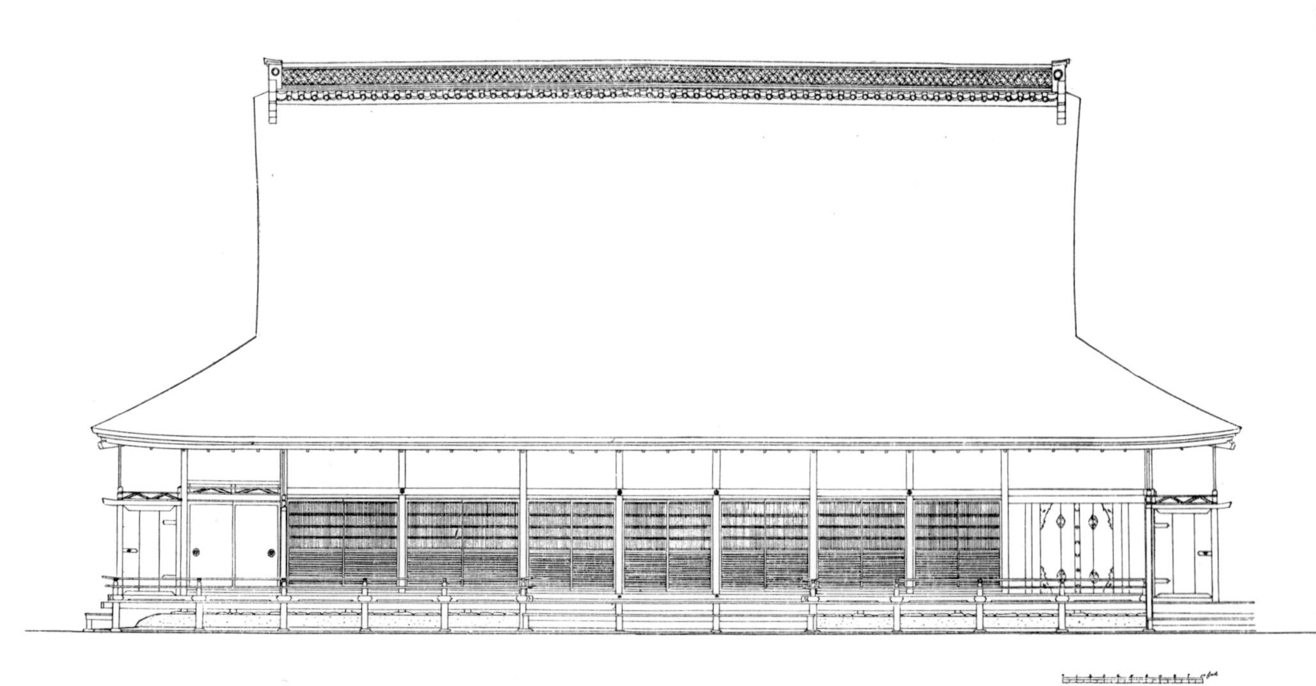

183. South Elevation.

The Hojo at Nanzen-ji

The Hojo of the Nanzen-ji represents a composite building. The front section was the former Seiryo-den of the Imperial Palace constructed by Hideyoshi, and the rear rooms came from Fushimi Castle. The cypress-bark roof of the entire building is in irimoya style.

The three rooms brought from Fushimi constitute the north-west section of the Hojo and are notable for the numerous paintings of tigers and bamboo done by Kano Tanyu on the gold backgrounds of the sliding doors. To the south of these Tiger Rooms, as they are called, is the Crane Room, which takes its name from its sliding-door decorations by Kano Eitoku. On the south side of the building are the West Room, the Midday Room, the Musk Room, and the Willow Room. The Midday Room is decorated with Kano Eitoku's portrayals of the Nijushiko, the Twenty-four Paragons of Filial Piety. The Willow Room and the Musk Room, as well as the small room

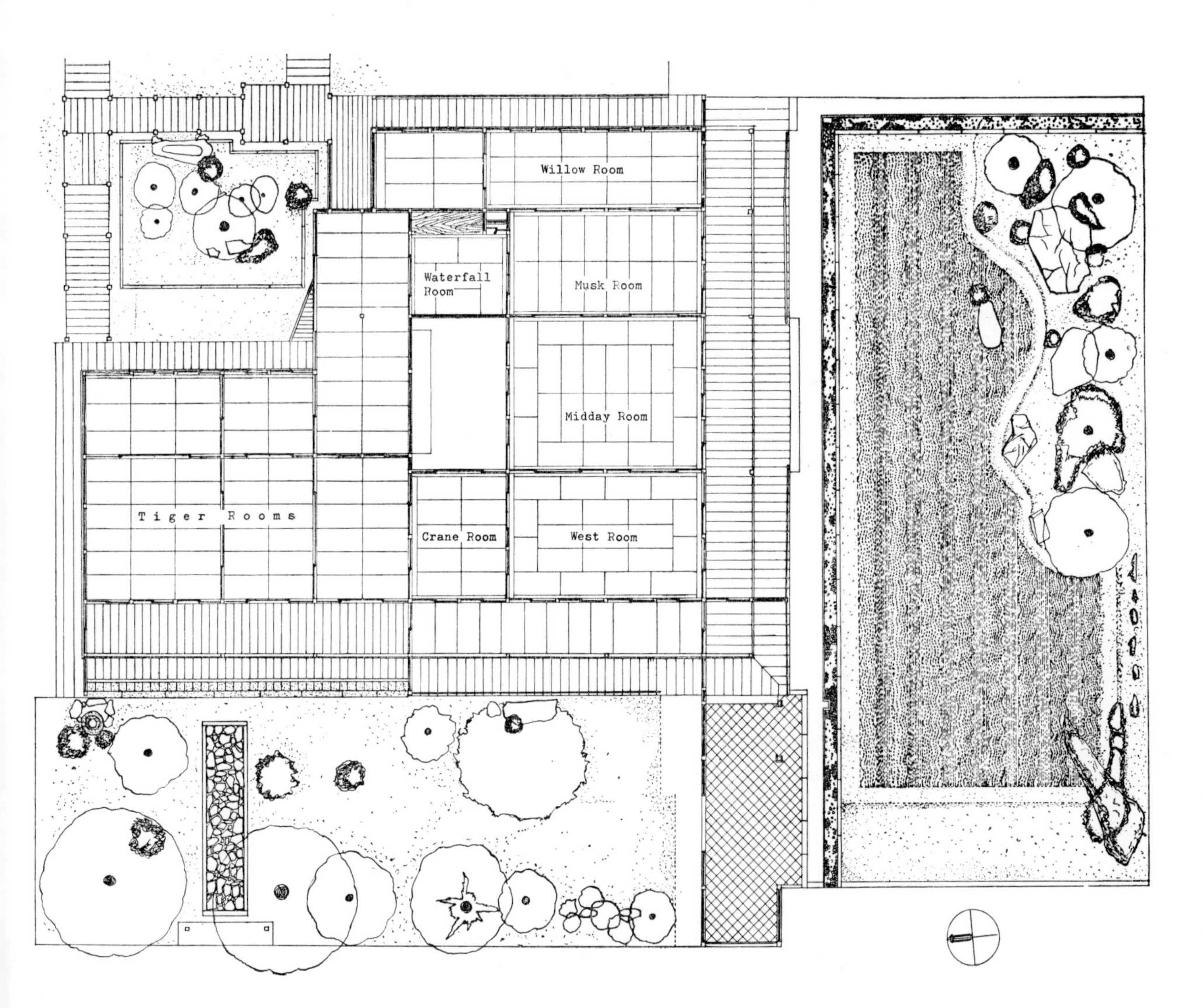

184. Plan.

to the north of the Willow Room, display paintings by Kano Motonobu. Behind the Midday Room is the altar.

The most interesting room in the Hojo is the Naritaki no Ma or Sounding Waterfall Room, named for its tokonoma painting by Kano Motonobu. It is a small room of only six mats which contains, in addition to its tokonoma, a small chigaidana.

The garden, attributed to Kobori Enshu, lies to the south of the building. It is composed of sand, bushes, trees, and a few carefully selected rocks.

185. Ceiling, Midday Room.

186. Shutters on East Side.

187. Railing, South Side.

188. Door Paintings by Kano Eitoku, Midday Room.

189. Tokonoma (left) and Chigaidana (center), Sounding Waterfall Room.

190. Sounding Waterfall Room.

191. Door Paintings by Kano Tanyu, First Tiger Room.

192. Door Paintings by Kano Tanyu, Third Tiger Room.

193. Door Paintings by Kano Eitoku, Crane Room.

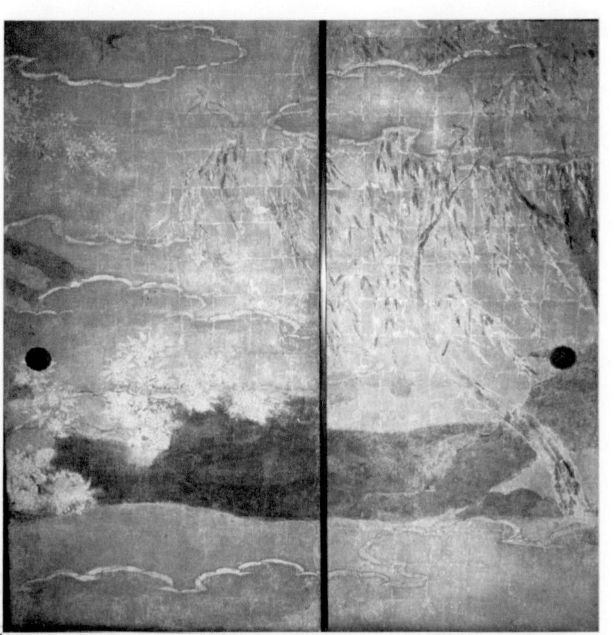

194. Door Paintings by Kano Motonobu, Willow Room.

195. Door Paintings by Kano Motonobu.

196. Door Paintings by Kano Motonobu, Musk Room.

■ 11 Jurakudai

■ HIDEYOSHI lived in Osaka Castle after its completion but found it inconvenient to be such a distance from Kyoto. He therefore decided to build a mansion in the capital, selecting a site which had once been occupied by the former Imperial Palace but which had been left in ruins since the Muromachi period. Ropes were stretched around the site, and construction was started in 1586. Large timbers for the buildings were gathered from as far away as Shikoku.

The residence was a palace, but its perimeter was heavily fortified in the manner of a castle. It was called Jurakudai or Palace of Pleasure. The area was to the northeast of the present Nijo Castle. Stone walls protected by deep moats were erected on all sides. Inside these walls were a number of enclosures containing individual mansions and gates. The buildings were decorated with gold, silver, and elaborate carvings. Along the four sides were houses built for Hideyoshi's generals and other subjects who had done meritorious deeds. The main tower was decorated with cloisonné, and the roofs were of gold-plated tiles, with dolphins adorning the ridges. The gardens of the palace contained rare trees and plants as well as a collection of the finest rocks. The main entrance was through a majestic two-storied iron gate embellished with iron birds, beasts, plants, and flowers.

After subjugating several warlords in Kyushu, Hideyoshi moved into Jurakudai in 1587. An ostentatious procession of palanquins, vehicles, mounted warriors, and bearers accompanied him to his new home.

In 1588, Hideyoshi requested that the emperor pay him a visit at Jurakudai. The custom of imperial visits to private resi-

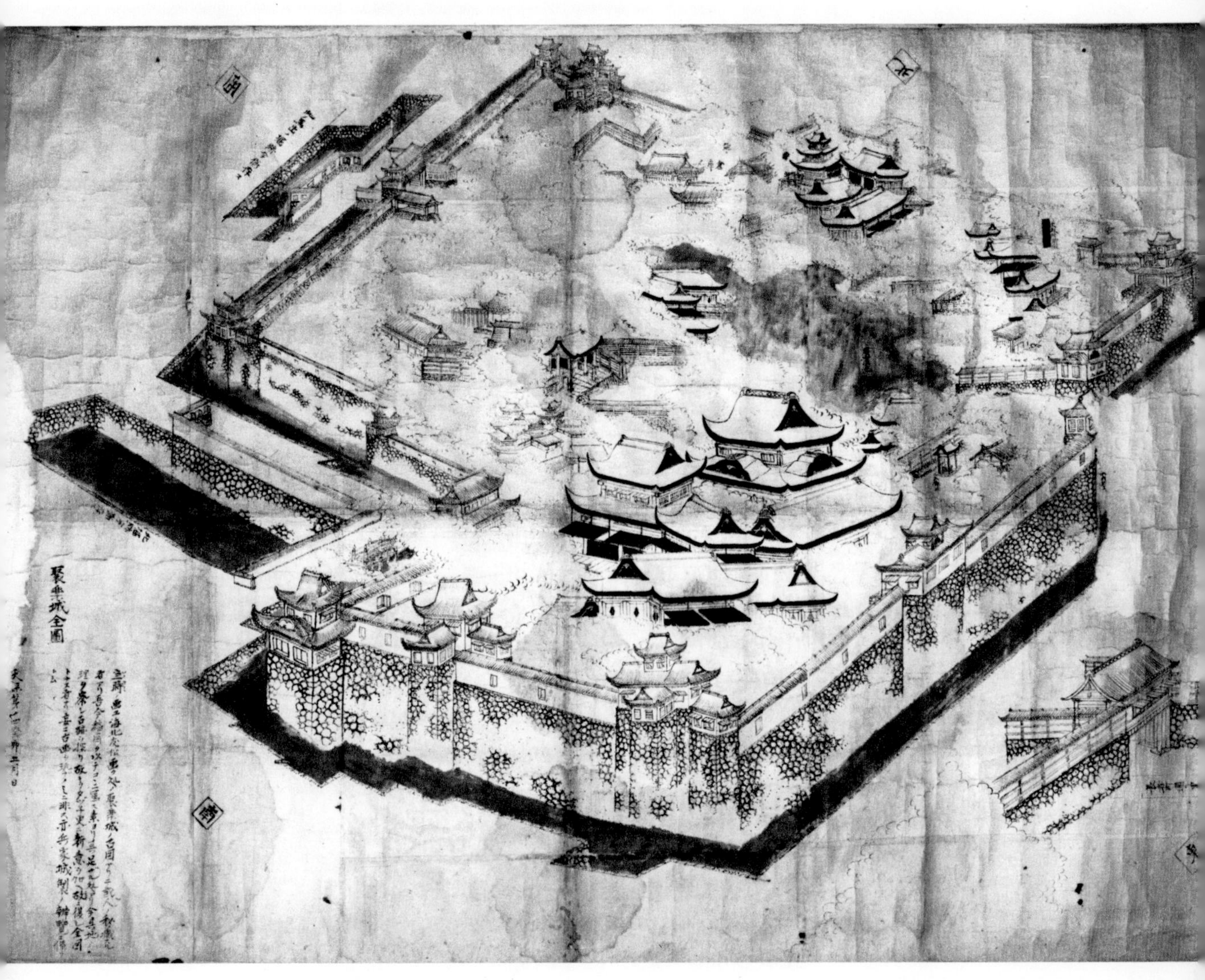

197. Jurakudai (from an original painting owned by Mrs. Jiro Kato).

dences had not been observed since the time of Ashikaga Yoshinori (1437), and Hideyoshi appointed his advisor, Maeda Gen-i, to study old records and plan for the reception of the emperor.

On the morning of the day appointed for the imperial visit, crowds of Kyoto citizens lined the route from the Imperial Palace to Jurakudai, a distance of about one mile. The emperor appeared in the South Hall of the palace and proceeded over a bridge upon which a carpet had been spread. Hideyoshi himself carried his train. The procession began with soldiers wearing Chinese hats. Behind them advanced some thirty palanquins bearing the empress, court ladies, and maids, all guarded by more than a hundred men. Next came the fifteen-odd palanquins of the princes of the blood, court nobles, and officials. These were followed by the imperial palanquin and those of high-ranking officials. Hideyoshi, his generals, and his warriors made up the rear. It is said that the beginning of the procession reached Jurakudai before the end had left the Imperial Palace.

Following the arrival of the retinue at Jurakudai, a large dinner party was given. After dinner the curtains at the western side of the hall were raised to reveal the sun setting over a garden filled with rare flowers and plants. The night was given to musical entertainment, and the emperor himself played the *koto,* a Japanese version of the harp. It is apparent that the emperor enjoyed the festivities, since the visit, which had been scheduled for three days, was extended to five.

On the second day, Hideyoshi offered the levies of all the ground in Kyoto to the emperor. Gifts were also presented to other members of the imperial family. At the same time, Hideyoshi required the daimyo in attendance to swear allegiance to the throne and to himself. After this, a poetry contest was held, and the emperor and all others of note among the guests composed poems. On the fourth day there was dancing and music, and more presents were made to the throne. Finally, on the fifth day, the emperor returned to the palace in a procession similar to that in which he had come. Its splendor was enhanced by the addition of some fifty lacquered chests covered with brocade and ornamented with the imperial crest. These contained the gifts that the emperor and his retinue had received.

In 1592, Hideyoshi resigned the office of kampaku (regent), which was then given to his adopted son, Hidetsugu. Jurakudai was to be Hidetsugu's official residence. But when Hidetsugu refused to accompany Hideyoshi to Nagoya (Kyushu) to prepare for the expedition against China—apparently because he preferred to stay at Jurakudai leading a life of leisure—Hideyoshi began to entertain suspicions about his loyalty. The birth of a real son in August of 1593 is said to be the real reason that Hideyoshi turned against Hidetsugu, but the matter is one of the mysteries buried in the history of this period. Hidetsugu was forced to commit suicide at Mt. Koya, and his head, together with those of his sons and more than thirty ladies from his household, was exhibited in the capital.

After the death of Hidetsugu, Hideyoshi ordered Jurakudai torn down. The structures were either moved to Fushimi Castle or given to temples in Kyoto. We are fortunate that one shoin-sukiya building, one gate, one teahouse, and one reconstructed teahouse are in existence to give us a glimpse of the Palace of Pleasure. There are also a few screen paintings which show portions of the palace.

The Gate at Daitoku-ji

From a distance, this gate of the karamon type appears to be very simple but when seen from close range it abounds in the ornate carvings of the period. The bark roof is supported by six round pillars, and the lintel extends outward to the sides of the gate, where it is topped by large Chinese lions (karashishi) at each end. Two large peacocks stand above the lintel in the central portion under the roof. The other beams are similarly covered with elaborate wood sculpture of dragons and other mythical creatures, waves, and branches of trees. The pillars, doors, beams, and gables are decorated with intricate metalwork that has lost its luster through the ages.

198. View from North.

199. Underside of South Gable.

200. Carving above Lintel.

201. West End of Lintel.

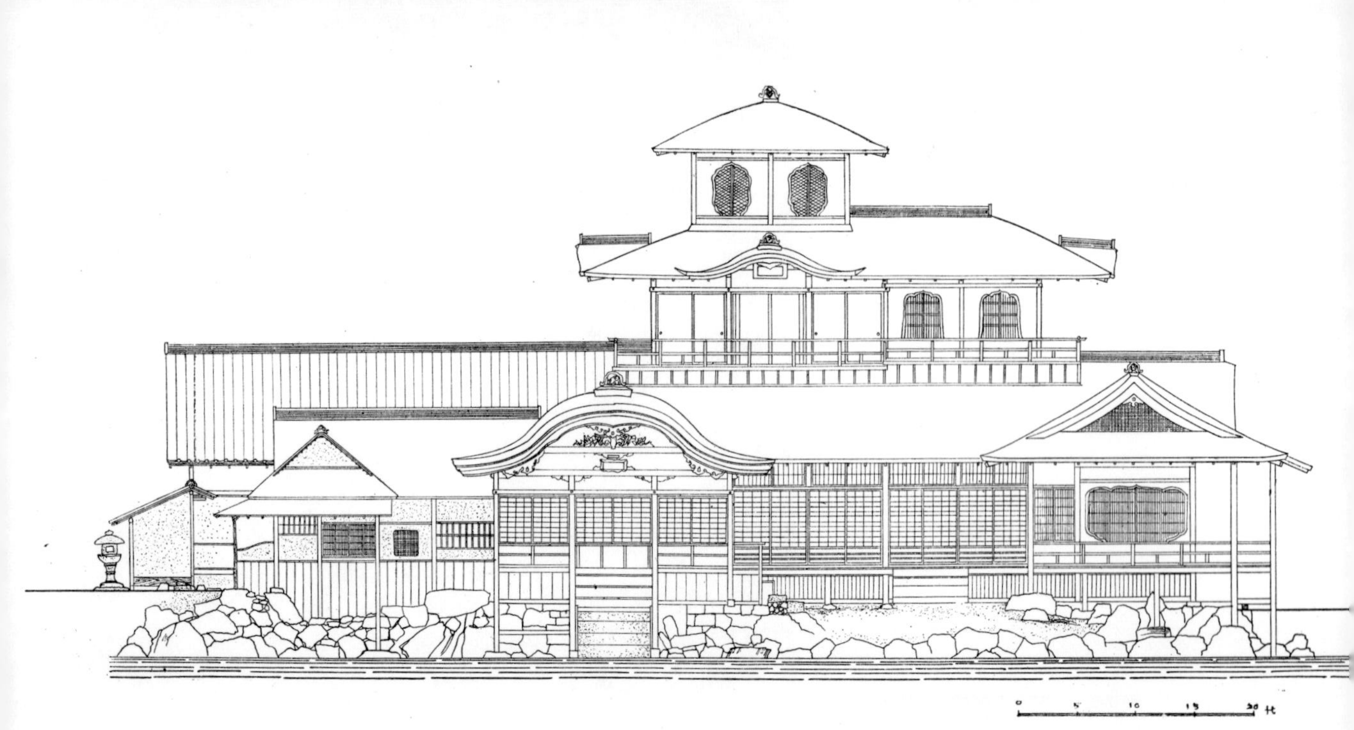

202. North Elevation.

The Hiun-kaku, Okujaku-tei, and Kokakudai of the Nishi Hongan-ji

The Hiun-kaku or Flying Cloud Pavilion, with its teahouse, the Okujaku-tei, and its bath, the Kokakudai, was probably removed from Jurakudai to Fushimi Castle. Upon the dismantling of the castle, the buildings were moved to the Tekisui garden of the Nishi Hongan-ji in 1615. The Hiun-kaku now stands at the edge of Soro Pond in this garden—the only existing building in the shoin-sukiya style of the Momoyama period. It is a three-storied structure whose asymmetric outside plan displays a harmonious blending of many different gables and shapes. The teahouse called Okujaku-tei is located at the northwest corner, while rooms of a later date are connected to the southwest portion. Only the first floor of the Hiun-kaku has been kept in good condition. The wood in the second and

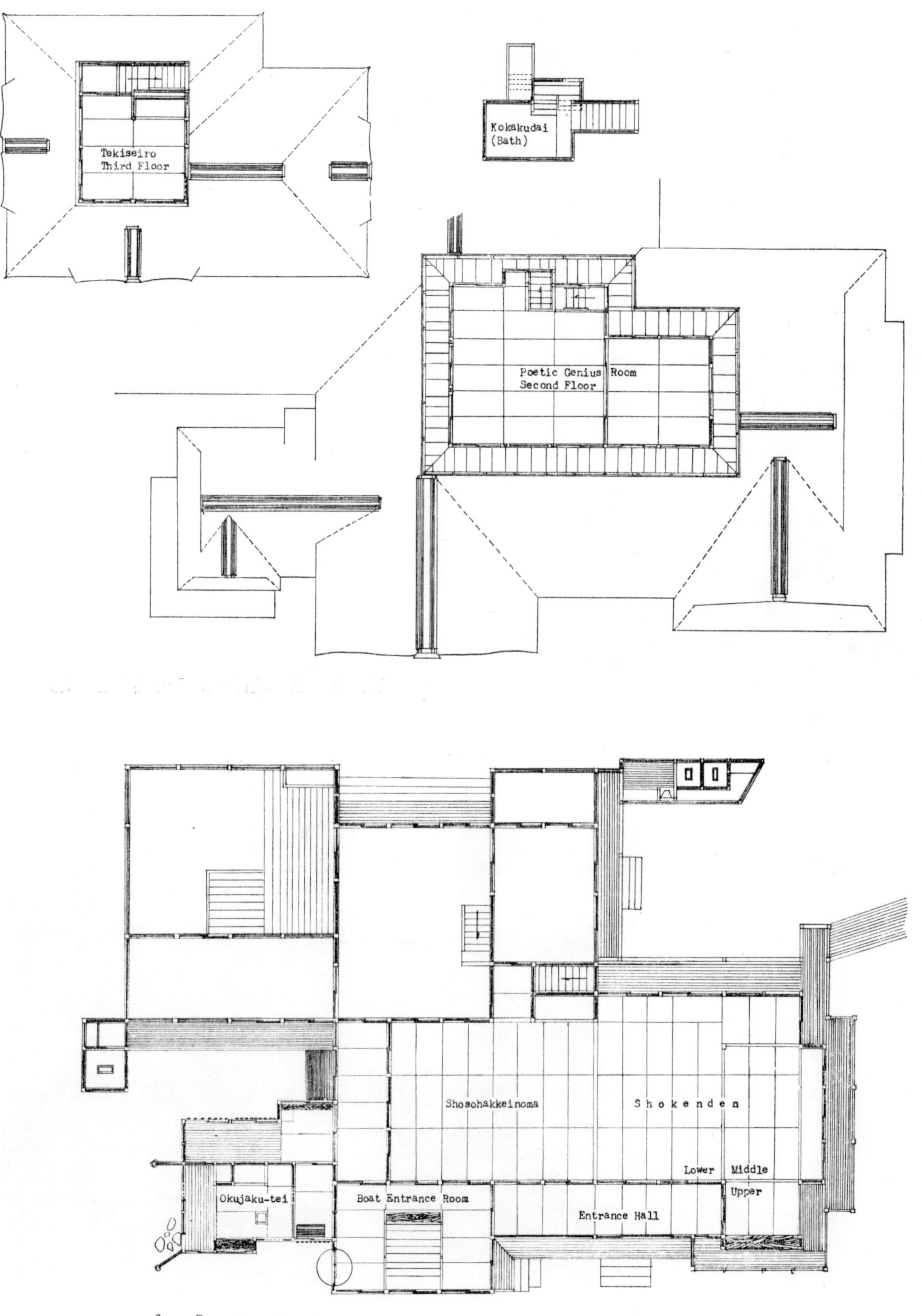
Tekiseiro
Third Floor
Kokakudai
(Bath)
Poetic Genius Room
Second Floor
Shosohakkeinoma
Shokenden
Lower
Middle
Upper
Okujaku-tei
Boat Entrance Room
Entrance Hall
0 5 10 15 20 feet

203. Plan.

204. Round Window, Funairi no Ma.

205. Boat Entrance, Funairi no Ma.

206. Second-Floor Porch, Okujaku-tei.

207. Outside Corner, Shoken-den.

208. Upper Section, Shoken-den.

209. Shoken-den.

210. North Side, Okujaku-tei.

211. Shoin-toko and Low Entrance, Okujaku-tei.

212. Section for Washing Utensils, Okujaku-tei.

213. Corridor, Okujaku-tei.

214. Low Entrance, Okujaku-tei.

215. Kasen no Ma, Okujaku-tei.

216. Tokonoma, Tekisei-ro, Okujaku-tei.

217. Corridor Leading to Kokakudai.

218. Crown Rack and Paintings by Kano Eitoku, Kokakudai.

219. Steam Bath, Kokakudai.

third floors is suffering from rot and destruction by insects and, because of this condition, these floors are closed off—an arrangement that is hastening their deterioration. The author, although he weighs 200 pounds, made it to the second and third floors without the structure's collapsing (which had been threatened), but had to take his photographs in almost complete darkness.

The first floor of the Hiun-kaku consists of an entrance hall and three rooms known as the Shoshohakkei no Ma, the Funairi no Ma, and the Shoken-den. The first of these, reached after one passes through the entrance hall, is a centrally located room with paintings by Kano Sanraku depicting the eight most beautiful views of Lake Hsiao-Hsiang in China. On the north side of the room is a tokonoma. To the left of the entrance hall is the Funairi no Ma or Boat Entrance Room, which contains a horizontally sliding trap door from which steps lead down to a boat in the pond. This arrangement is said to have been an escape route for Hideyoshi. In the east wall of the room is a round window.

To the west of the entrance hall and adjacent to the Shoshohakkei no Ma is the Shoken-den, which consists of a lower section or *gedan,* a middle section or *chudan,* and an upper section or *jodan.* The upper section, done in the tsukeshoin style, contains a large bell-shaped window. The middle section juts out into the room and is backed by an elevated alcove much like a tokonoma, except that it contains shoji windows. On the east side of the room are sliding doors decorated with paintings of willows in snow by Kano Eitoku.

The Okujaku-tei, the teahouse in the northeast corner of the Hiun-kaku can be entered from the Hiun-kaku proper or from a low entrance on the east side. The principal room is of three and a third mats plus a tokonoma and a *shoin-toko*—that is, a tsukeshoin resembling a tokonoma. One pillar of the tokonoma is the trunk of a palm tree. A room for washing and storing utensils lies to the northwest and a corridor to the south provides another exit to the outside.

The Kasen no Ma (Hall of the Famous Poets) on the second floor derives its name from the Kano Sanraku paintings of the Thirty-six Famous Poets that decorate its wooden sliding doors. Paintings of squirrels and grapevines by the same artist adorn the ceiling. The room contains a lower section of 16 2/3 mats plus an elevated section of 8 mats and is surrounded on all sides by an open porch with a low railing. On the third floor is the Tekisei-ro, a room of 7 2/3 mats plus a tokonoma. The rear wall of the tokonoma is embellished with a painting, now barely visible, called the Suwari Fuji (Sitting Fuji) and attributed to Kano Motonobu. Its odd name derives from the fact that it can be properly appreciated only from a sitting position. The bottom of this picture has paintings of pine trees which legend indicates were added by Hideyoshi. The pillar of the tokonoma is of azalea wood, and the windows of the room are in the shape of fans.

The Kokakudai or bath consists of a six-mat upper anteroom and a lower section which contains two types of baths. This building is connected with the Hiun-kaku by a covered corridor. The upper room, decorated by Kano Eitoku, contains a crown rack. Stairs purposely designed to squeak lead down to the bathroom. To the south of this lower room is a *mushiburo* or steam bath covered by a curved Chinese gable, and to the north are baths for hot and cold water. To the east is an escape door. Near this bath is the toilet supposedly used by Hideyoshi; even though it is a national treasure, it is kept locked.

The Chinryu-tei at the Sambo-in

It is thought that this teahouse was once part of Jurakudai. The building was probably given to the Sambo-in after Jurakudai was dismantled in 1595 and before Hideyoshi's death in 1598.

The teahouse now has a thatched roof, although I have seen old pictures of the Chinryu-tei which showed that the upper portion of the thatched roof was covered with tile. (The roof can be seen at a distance in Figure 28.)

The north room is a three-mat tearoom for special guests. It is slightly higher than the other rooms and has its own entrance

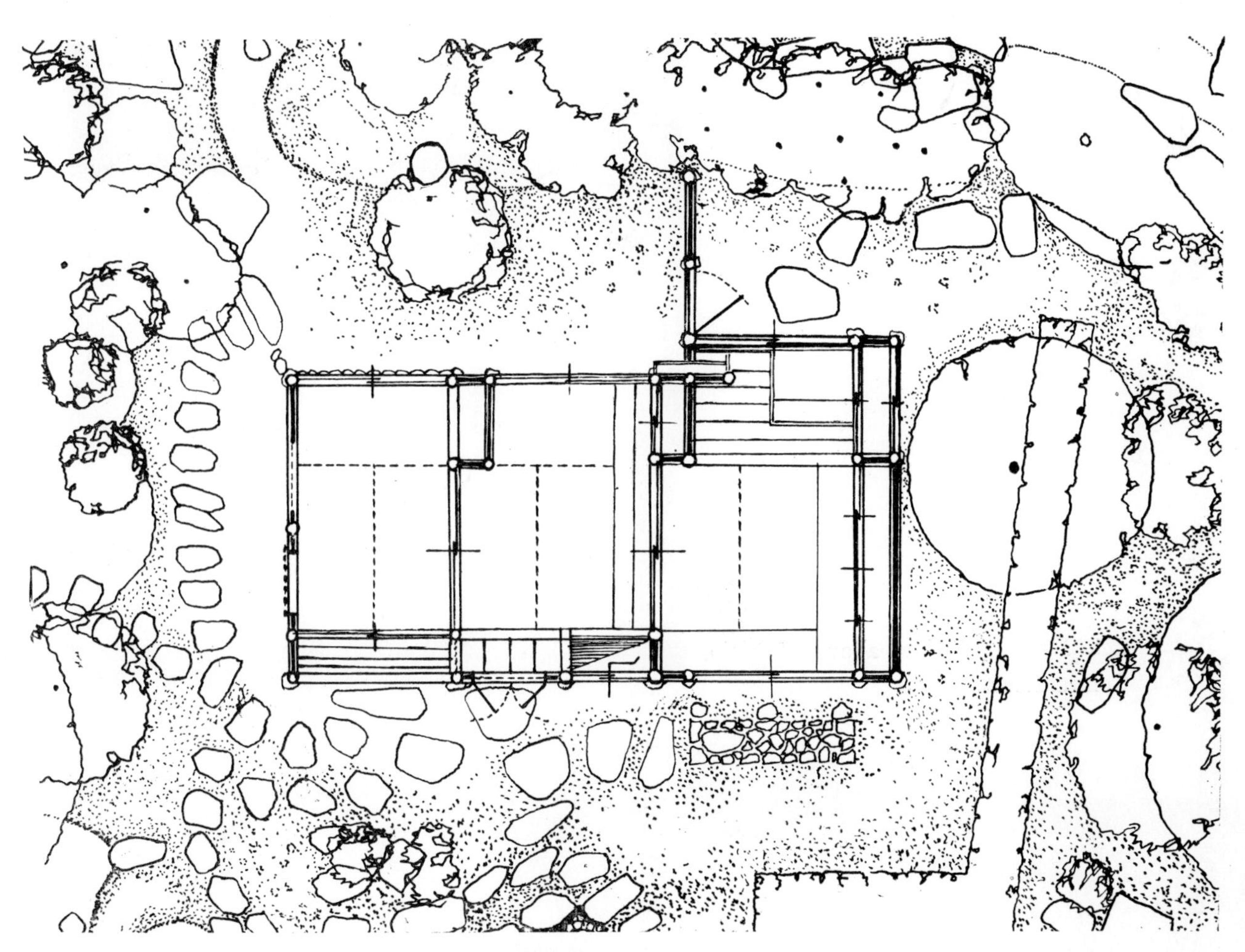

220. Plan.

and tokonoma. The central room of 2 2/3 mats is entered from the outside through two hinged doors (mairado) above which is a circular window. Next to these doors is a mizuya with an interesting arrangement of shelves. These rooms give fine views of the garden to the east.

The south room is technically a two-mat room, although the mats are surrounded by a narrow floor of boards. On the east side, it has an entrance whose base is at ground level and extends into the room.

221. Round Window above Mairado, Central Room.

222. Entrance to North Room.

223. Entrance to South Room.

224. Tokonoma, North Room.

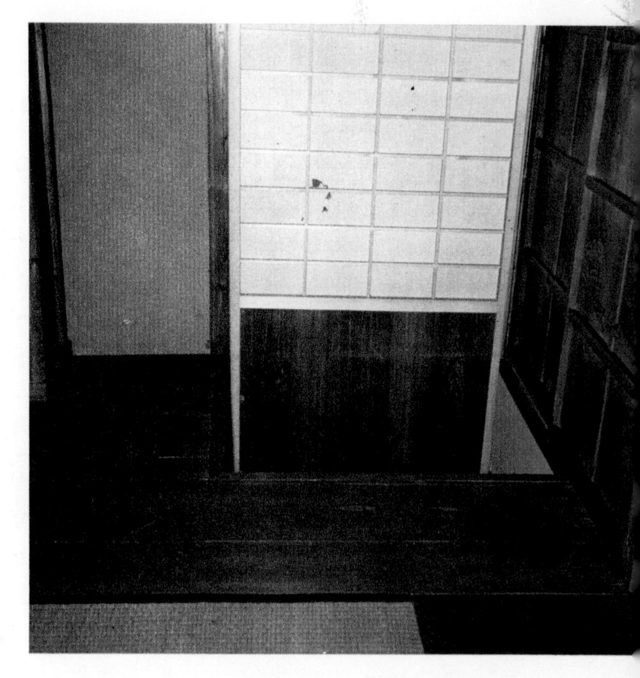

225. Mizuya.

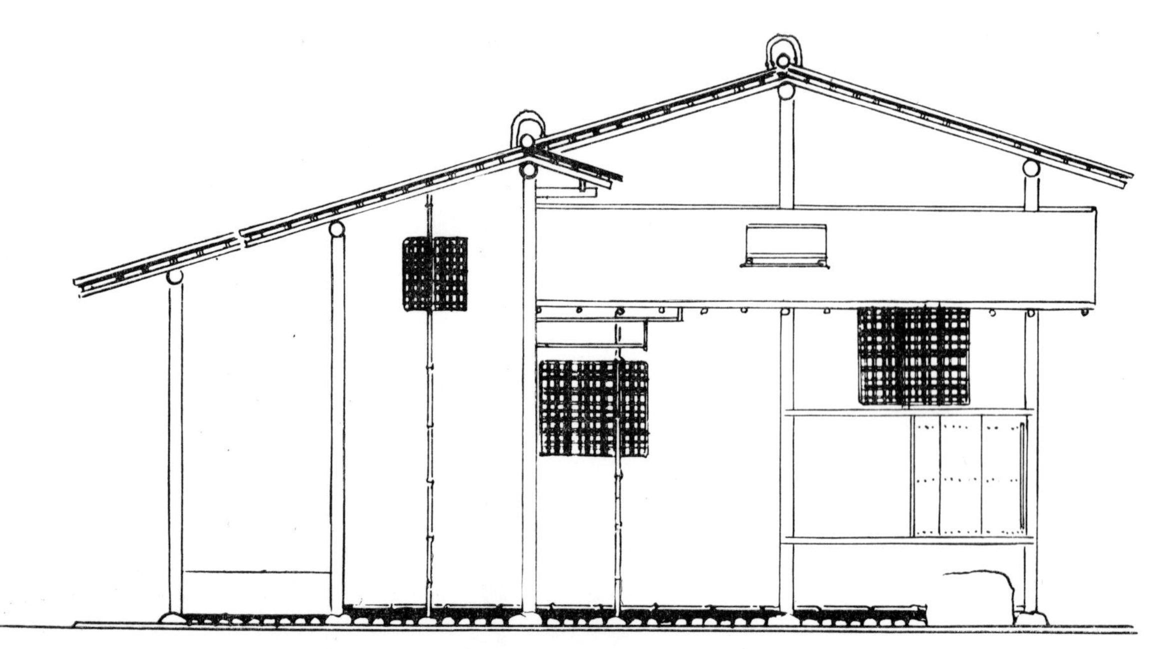

226. North Elevation.

The Fushin-an at Omote-Senke

The Fushin-an was built by the famous tea master Sen no Rikyu for Jurakudai. When the palace was dismantled, the teahouse was given to him. In 1591, out of anger at Sen's increasing arrogance and insubordination, Hideyoshi ordered him to commit suicide, and the Fushin-an was probably destroyed at that time. Sen no Rikyu's grandson, Shoan, constructed a duplicate of the teahouse at the present site. Unfortunately, the Fushin-an has been destroyed by fire several times since Shoan rebuilt it, although it has always been reconstructed after the original—the last time in 1923. It is now used by the head of one of the three schools of the tea ceremony founded by Sen no Rikyu's sons. The present tea master is Sokuchusai, a descend-

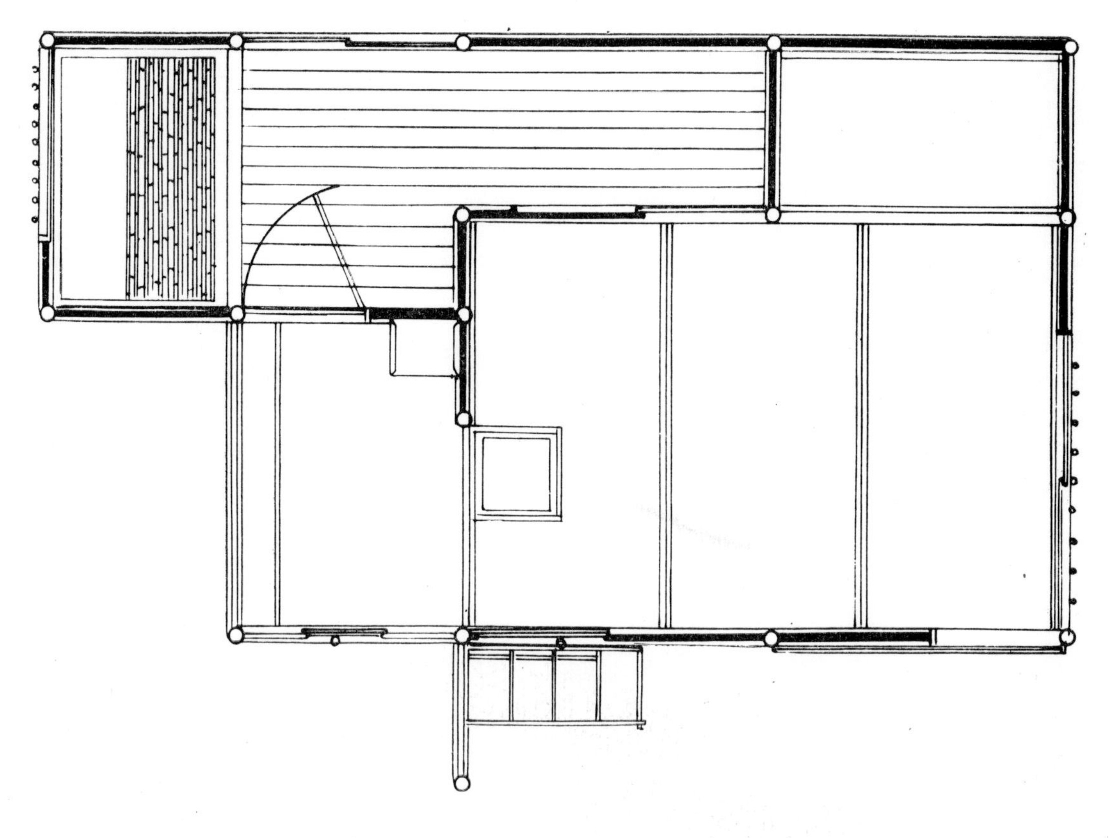

227. Plan.

ant of Sen no Rikyu in the thirteenth generation. Although the teahouse is comparatively new, it is important because it is representative of Sen no Rikyu's work.

The Fushin-an is one of the few Momoyama-period teahouses that still retain an outside waiting bench of original design. The teahouse itself is entered through a low door on the south side and consists of a 3 3/4-mat room. On the west wall is a tablet bearing the name of the teahouse. Below this is an area partially separated by a wall with an open lower section and a pillar. On the north side of the room are a tokonoma, a door for servants, and the host's entrance. There is a place for washing and storing utensils to the north of the tearoom.

228. Outside Waiting Bench.

229. Sword Rack.

230. Low Entrance.

231. West Section of Tearoom, Fushin-an.

232. Name Tablet and Section of Ceiling.

233. East Section.

■ 12 Independent Structures

■ THE EXAMPLES of existing structures from the Momoyama period which we have thus far examined have come from complexes such as castles and palaces. Buildings of an independent nature have also survived. In most cases these buildings were contributed to or constructed by Buddhist temples. We are particularly indebted to these temples for the care and preservation of historical architecture rendered through the ages by countless generations of devotees.

The Omote-shoin at the Sambo-in

Daigo, located a few miles south of Fushimi, is noted for its beautiful cherry blossoms. Once when Hideyoshi was in the area to view the blossoms, the priest of the Sambo-in pleaded for aid to restore his temple. Hideyoshi complied with the request and personally helped to plan one of the gardens. The Omote-shoin, which faces on this garden, was probably constructed shortly before Hideyoshi's death in 1598.

The building consists of three rooms surrounded by porches and corridors. A porch with an upper and a lower section faces the garden to the south and juts out towards it at the southwest corner. The roof is of tile. The west room, known as the Agebutai Room (Stage Room) because it was often used in former times for the presentation of Kabuki plays, is lower than the other two, and the awkward joining of the beams and the paintings of peacocks and pines by Ishida Yutei (1721–86) seem to indicate that it is of later date. The metal fittings on

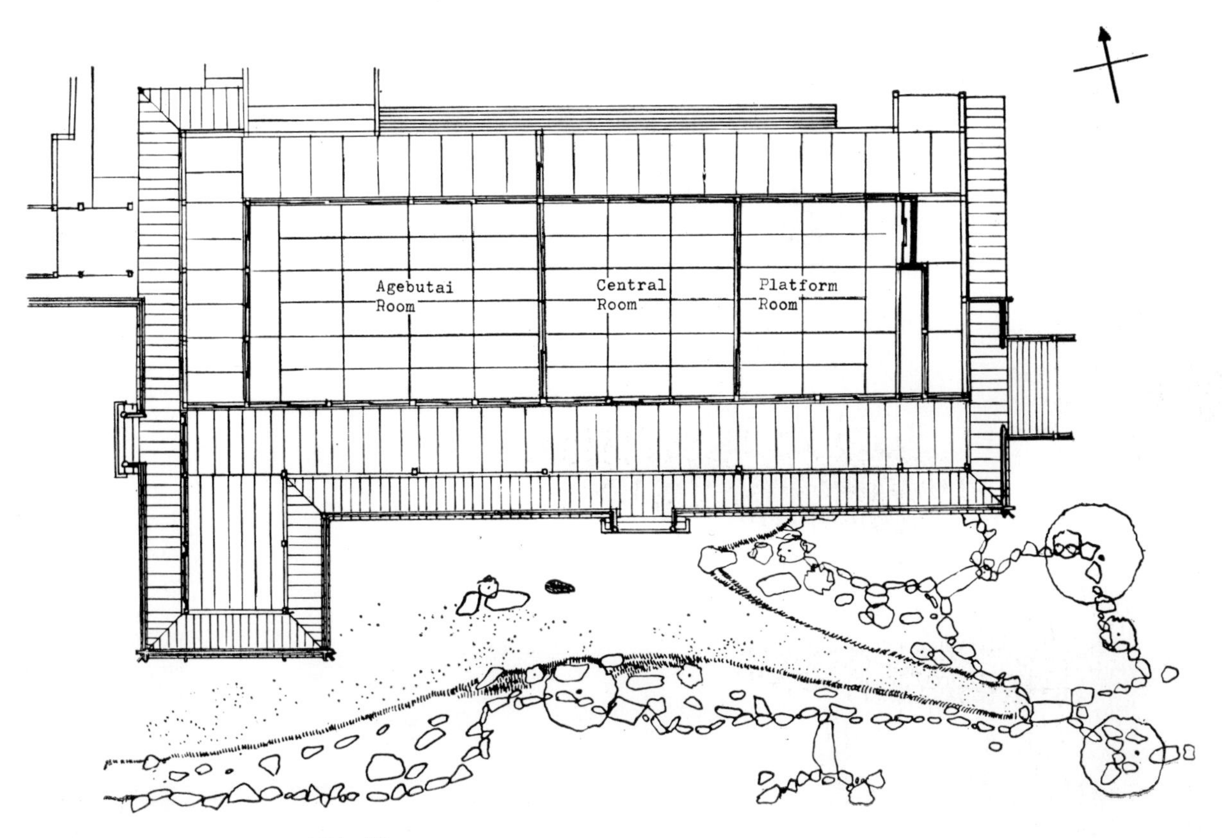

234. Plan.

the steps leading to the central room are unique. The room itself has sliding doors decorated with paintings of plants and trees by Kano Sanraku. To the east is the Jodan no Ma (Platform Room). Although the room itself is not elevated, it was probably intended to contain a small platform for Hideyoshi's use. On the east side is an unusually large tokonoma with a painting of a pine tree. The chigaidana and the sliding doors carry paintings of willows, also by Kano Sanraku.

Hideyoshi laid out the garden of the Omote-shoin in March of 1598, employing gardeners from Fushimi Castle for the work. But he died during the same year, and the garden was

235. West View.

236. South Porch.

237. East View of Porch.

238. Detail of Door Frames, Agebutai Room.

239. Sliding Shutters.

240. Door Paintings by Ishida Yutei, Agebutai Room.

241. Painted Cedar Doors.

242. Chigaidana and Paintings by Kano Sanraku, Platform Room.

243. Tokonoma, Platform Room.

not completed until 1615. It occupies a rectangular space 180 by 80 feet on the south side of the building and has for its basic features a background of hills and a lake fed by two cascades. In the lake are three islands linked by bridges, two of which are of stone and one of wood topped with moss-covered earth. The garden displays a large number of stones—among them the Fujito Stone, which was brought from Jurakudai. Tall, square in cross section, and pock-marked, it serves as the "guardian" stone of the garden and is considered to be the most famous stone in Japan. It is said to possess supernatural powers, and throughout Japanese history it has been successively featured in the finest gardens. Tradition says that it was always wrapped in brocade and accompanied by music whenever it was moved.

The Toyobo at Kennin-ji

In 1587, Hideyoshi gave a magnificent tea party at Kitano in Kyoto. People of all classes from Kyoto and neighboring cities were invited to attend, and the important tea masters all designed teahouses to be exhibited on this occasion. Hideyoshi himself put his most precious tea bowls and utensils on display. The Toyobo was the teahouse entered in this exhibit by Toyobo Sochin, a pupil of Sen no Rikyu. It was later transferred to the Kennin Temple.

The teahouse has low entrances on both the west and the north sides. The principal room, which is on the south side, is of 2 2/3 mats and contains a tokonoma and a wall with an open lower section and a curved pillar. The lack of a visible corner post in the northeast corner is of interest. The east wall of the room to the north has a round window. The western wing was added at a later date and contains washing and cooking areas and a door to the outside.

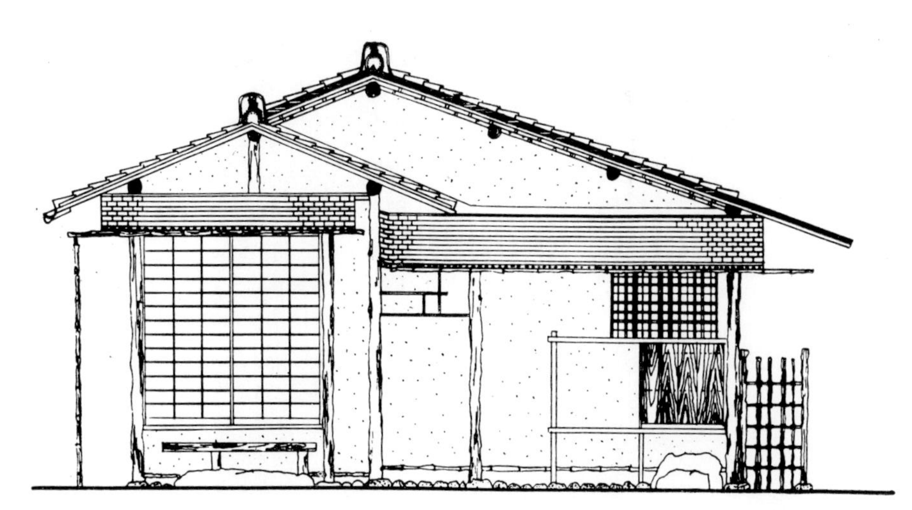

244. West Elevation.

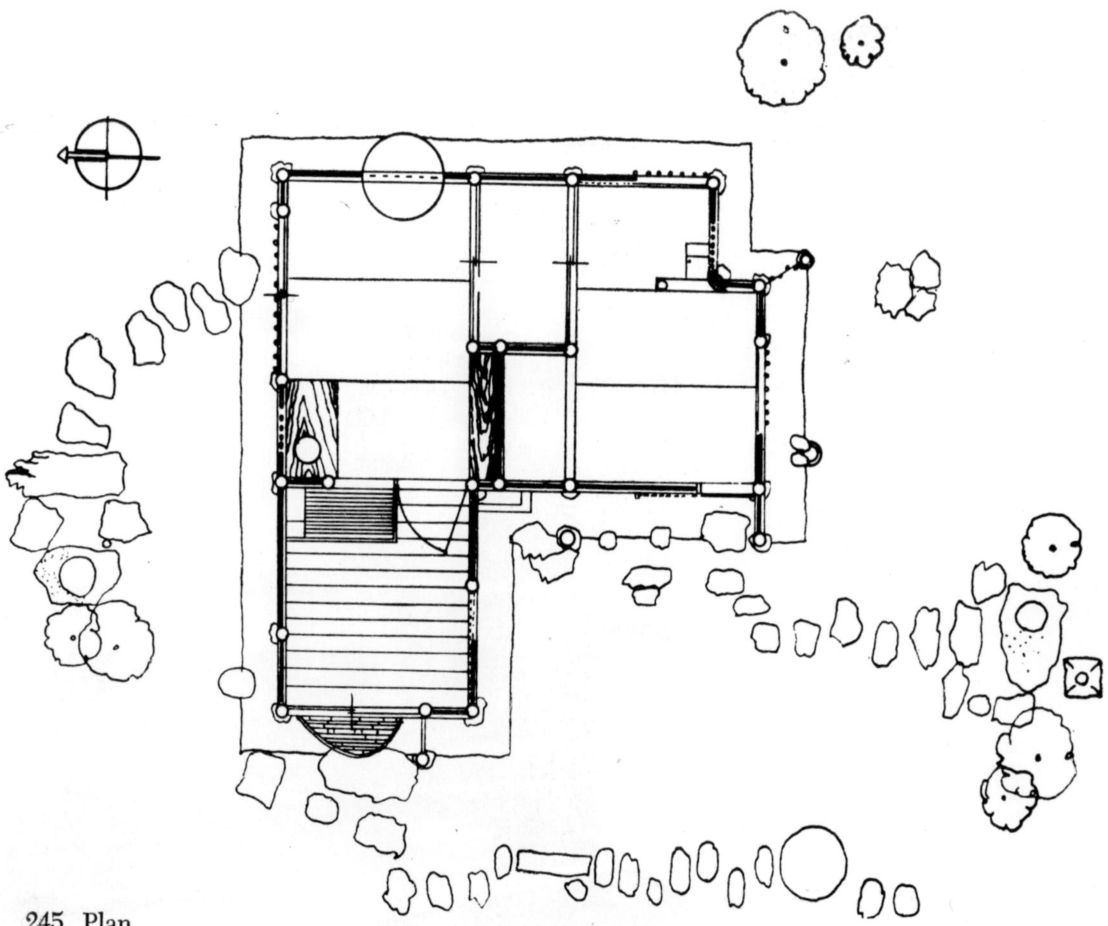

245. Plan.

246. Low Entrance on West Side.

247. Inside View of Low Entrance on West Side.

248. Low Entrance on North Side.

249. Inside View of Low Entrance on North Side.

250. Entrance to West Wing.

251. Curved Pillar and Open Wall.

252. Northeast Corner.

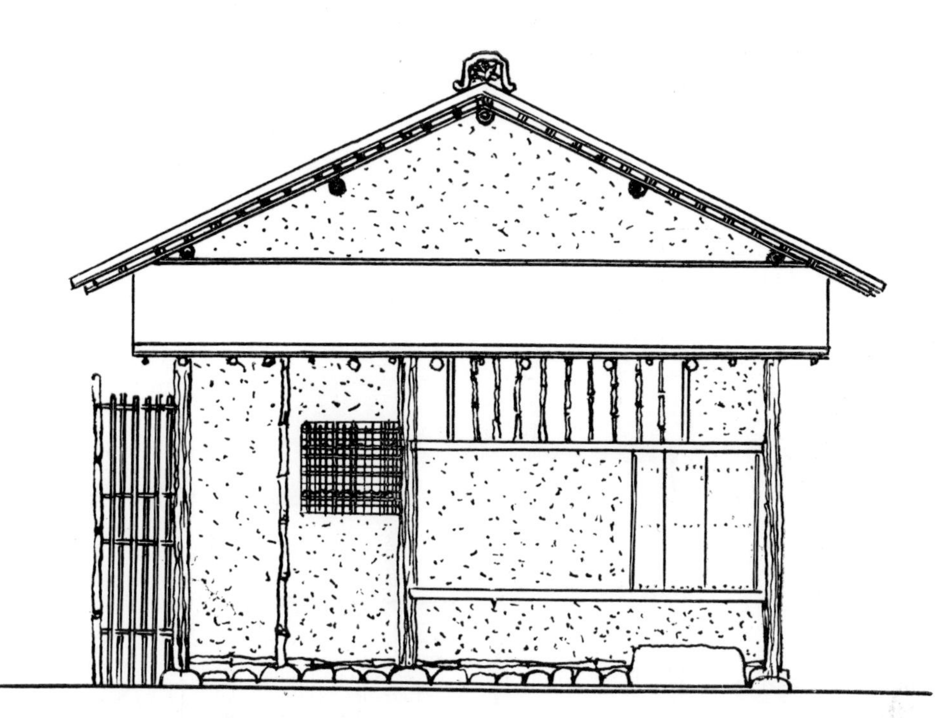

253. South Elevation.

The Tai-an at the Myoki-an

In 1582, Sen no Rikyu built a small teahouse at Myoki-an, Yamazaki. At this time, Hideyoshi was engaged in battle in this area, and it is said that he and Sen no Rikyu often came here to enjoy the tea ceremony. The Tai-an is an example of the smallest type of tearoom. The room contains one mat for the host and one mat for the guest.

The Tai-an is entered through a low door on the south side. Legend has it that this entrance was made larger than usual to permit Hideyoshi to pass through it with his armor on. Across from it, in the main two-mat room, is a tokonoma. Near the ceiling on the west wall is a tablet bearing the name of the teahouse. To the west of the main room is a one-mat area which has a shelf for utensils. The teahouse is connected to an older building on the north side.

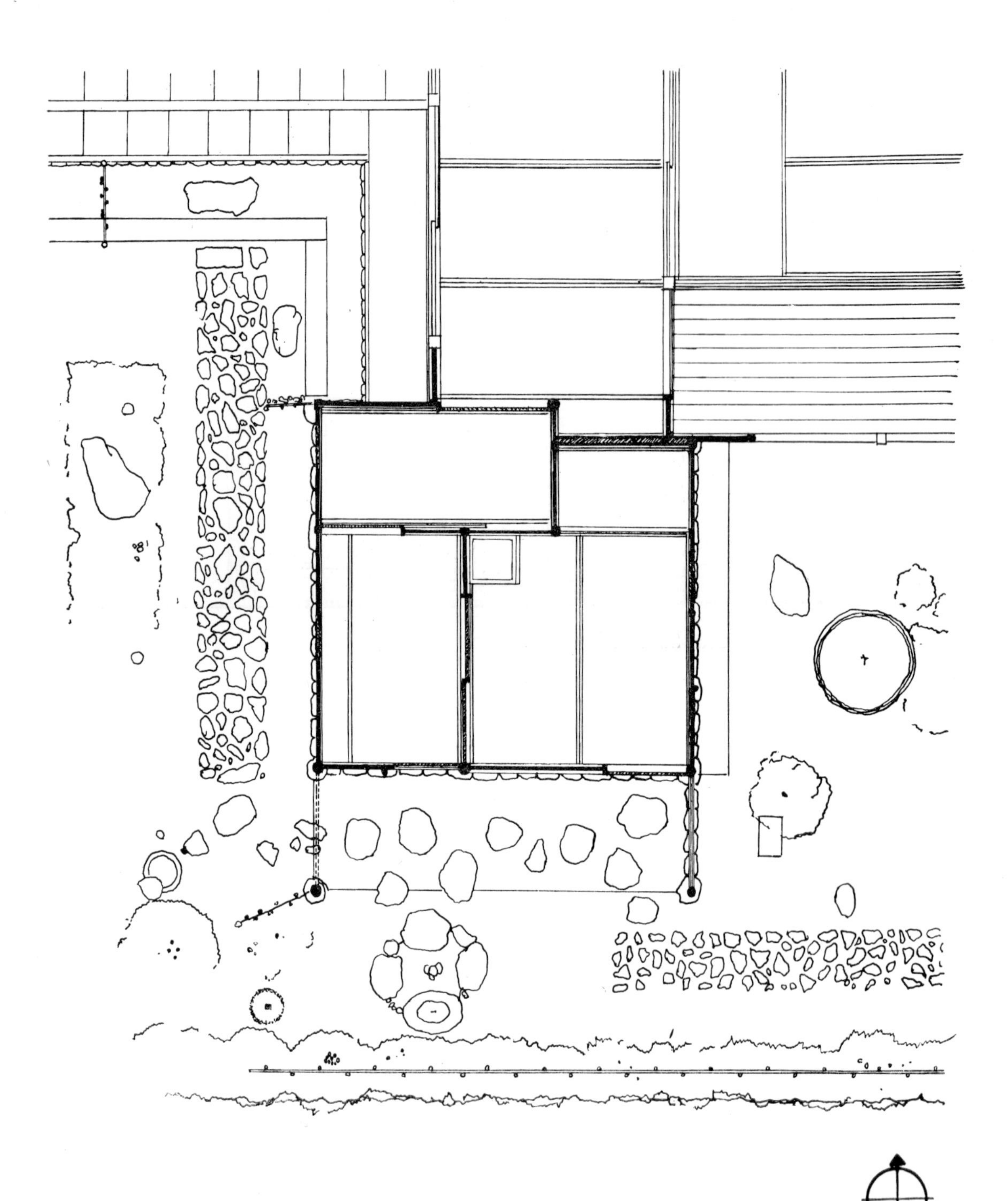

254. Plan.

255. Name Tablet and Section of Ceiling.

256. Low Entrance.

257. Shelf for Utensils.

258. Tokonoma.

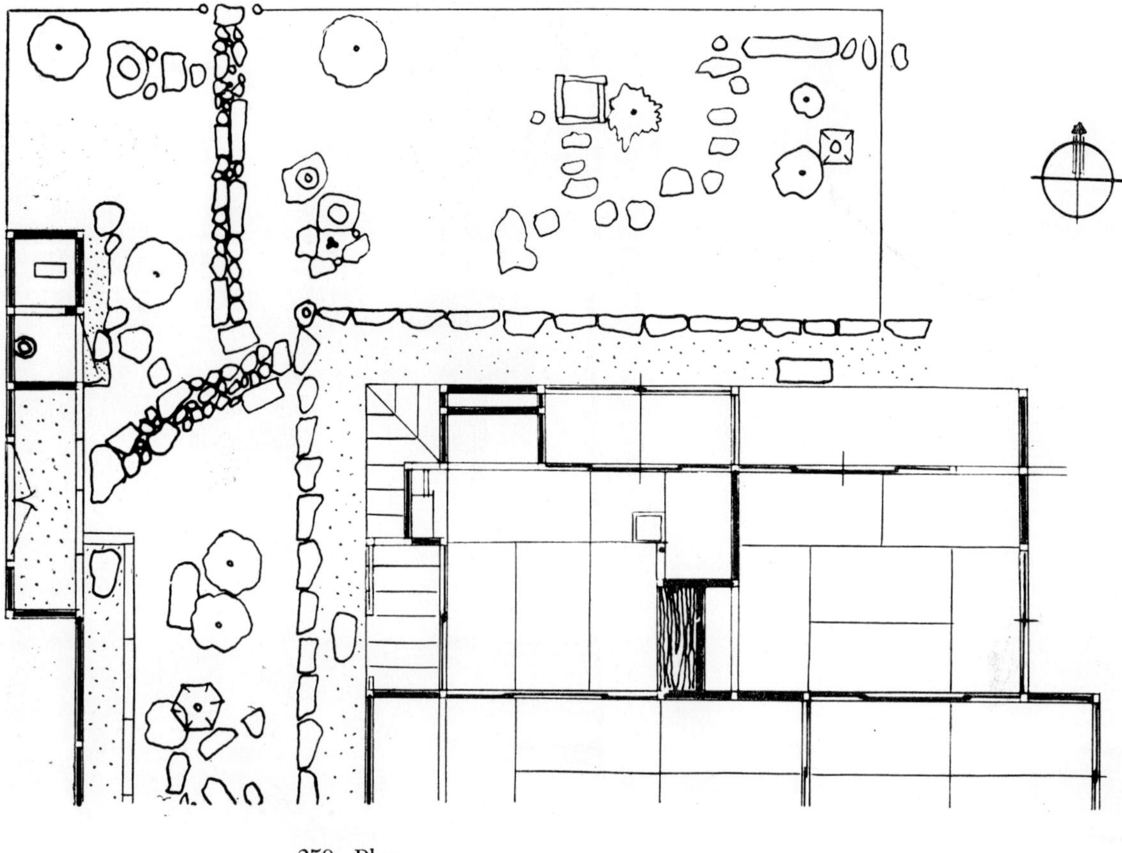

259. Plan.

The Ryoko-in at Daitoku-ji

The Ryoko-in (also called Mittan) was built at the Daitoku-ji between 1606 and 1608 by Kobori Enshu. Enshu is best known for the gardens which he designed in the late Momoyama and early Tokugawa periods. This teahouse is unique in that it is an attempt to reduce shoin architecture to a teahouse style. The wall paintings, the use of two tokonoma in one room, the enclosure with shelves, and the straight pillars are not usually found in teahouse architecture.

The entrance through sliding shoji doors is on the west side and includes a small porch with a railing. To the north of the entrance on this porch is a small partition behind which a guard could be stationed. On the west side of the five-mat

260. Porch with Hiding Place for Guard.

tearoom is an alcove with shelves; on the north, a deep tokonoma next to a small porch which can be concealed by shoji; and on the east, a shallow tokonoma and a wall with an open lower section. The dado of the sliding shoji doors is decorated with groups of three horizontal strips. The landscape paintings are by Kano Tanyu.

261. North Section.

262. Tokonoma and Chigaidana.

263. Area for Preparing Tea.

■ 13 Other Forms

■ THE BUILDING of religious edifices in the Momoyama period was largely concerned with the reconstruction of destroyed temples and shrines according to their original plans. However, a few shrines and temples were erected which reflect the general trend of the period and offer slight innovations. In the more spectacular vein was the construction of a colossal Buddhist image and a structure housing it which were first built by Hideyoshi and later reconstructed by his son. They were copied from earlier designs and have been entirely destroyed. Edifices were also constructed or converted for Christian worship in and around Kyoto, but little knowledge of these has survived.

In conclusion, two works of an engineering nature are included because they reflect the nature of the period and were undertakings of considerable achievement. The first was the construction by Hideyoshi of a large-scale bridge across the Kamo River. The other feat of almost Herculean proportions was the erection by Hideyoshi of an earthen embankment around the capital city of Kyoto.

The Hoko-ji

Inspired by the Great Buddhas of Nara (8th century) and Kamakura (13th century), Hideyoshi was determined to leave for posterity a Buddhist statue connected with his name. It was typical of his character that he should require the image to be larger than either of its predecessors. Construction was started in the eastern section of Kyoto in 1586. Maeda Gen-i was appointed to supervise the work, and he chose for his consultants two brothers from Nara, Teiso and Soin, who were experts in the making of Buddhist statues.

Since the scale for the building was very large, it was not easy to find sufficient timbers. Twenty-eight magistrates and twenty carpenters were dispatched to the various provinces to look for materials. Suitable logs were shipped from as far away as Kyushu and Shikoku. Workers, requisitioned from all the nearby provinces for the project, were divided into three sections, the first of which was engaged in leveling the ground, the second in erecting the stone walls, and the third in making artificial mounds. The area was 260 yards from east to west and 274 yards from north to south, and the hall to house the statue occupied a space 74 by 110 yards. Originally, the image was to be made of copper, but sufficient workmen were not available, and to hasten the project, Hideyoshi decided to construct it of wood and lacquer. At that time an expert in creating large images was staying in Kyushu during a visit from Ming China. He was quickly sent for and made an advisor in the work. The height of the hall was to be 200 feet and that of the Buddha 160 feet. Ten thousand bales of oyster shells were requisitioned for use in the lacquering process. Hideyoshi, becoming impatient, also sent for Mokujiki Shonin, a famous builder on Mt. Koya. Mokujiki, who established himself in a hut at the site of the project, is said to have speeded up the work.

An artificial hill was built on the east side of the area for righting the beams. Dissatisfied with the small stones used in the foundation, Hideyoshi ordered the daimyo to compete in contributing larger ones. The search for a timber large enough to form the ridgepole ended only when one was located near Mt. Fuji. Ieyasu was instructed to cut it down and ship it to Osaka, and it is reported that it took 50,000 men to do the job. To secure metal for the many nails and clamps to be used, Hideyoshi ordered all farmers to turn in their swords, spears, and other weapons. This means of disarming the masses under the pretense of contributing to religious salvation was not initiated by Hideyoshi; it had been used twice before in China with much success.

At the west of the area was the Nio Gate, from each side of which ran corridors that formed a square with the Daibutsu-den (Hall of the Great Buddha) in the center. The image, 160 feet in height, far surpassed those at Nara ($53\frac{1}{2}$ feet) and Kamakura

($42\frac{1}{2}$ feet). The dedication ceremony was performed by a thousand priests in 1589.

The Hoko-ji, however, survived for only seven years, since it was destroyed in the great earthquake of 1596. After Hideyoshi's death in 1598, Hideyori issued orders for the construction of another wooden image, but in 1603 a fire broke out in the scaffolding of the hall, and what had been completed went up in smoke.

Tokugawa Ieyasu, in pursuance of his policy of weakening Hideyori, persuaded him to construct still another image. The hall designed to house it was 150 feet in height, 272 in length, and $167\frac{1}{2}$ in depth. The roof was supported by 92 pillars varying in diameter from $4\frac{1}{2}$ to $5\frac{1}{2}$ feet and bound with iron bands. The seated figure of the Buddha was $58\frac{1}{2}$ feet high.

In 1614, just as a thousand priests were about to dedicate the temple, mounted messengers from Ieyasu appeared on the scene with orders to stop the ceremony. The spectators, who had assembled from all over the country for the dedication festivities, were so infuriated at the interruption that they broke into disorder and sacked part of the city. It turned out that Ieyasu had taken personal offense at the inscription on the bell of the edifice. This inscription, which to the ordinary eye read "Kokka anko" or "May the state be peaceful and prosperous," contained two characters, *ka* and *ko*, which can also be read *ie* and *yasu* or, taken together, Ieyasu. Interpreting this as a derogatory reflection upon himself, Ieyasu used it as a pretext for his assault on Hideyori. The bell, which is nearly 14 feet high and weighs over 63 tons, is one of the two largest in Japan. Its companion is at the Chion-in in Kyoto.

Hideyori's Great Buddha was destroyed in an earthquake in 1662. Repairs were made, and the wooden image was replaced with a bronze one. But the temple was struck by lightning in 1775 and again in 1798 and was thus completely destroyed. There remains, however, a scroll picture of the edifice as it once appeared. In 1843, a rich merchant from Osaka donated to the Hoko-ji a wooden image of much smaller size to take the place of the destroyed bronze one.

The buildings of the Hoko-ji presented no new architectural developments, for they were merely copies of older Chinese-style buildings. The original Daibutsu-den, however, was probably one of the largest wooden buildings ever created.

Across the road from the Hoko-ji is the Mimizuka or Ear Mound, beneath which were buried the ears and noses of the Koreans and Chinese killed in Hideyoshi's expeditions of 1592 and 1597. Although it was customary to bring home the entire heads of slain enemies, in this case, because the heads numbered 30,000 and thus created an insoluble shipping problem, only the ears or noses (the records say the noses, but the name of the burial place is the Ear Mound) were pickled in salt and shipped home.

Namban-ji

The records concerning the names, locations, and dates of the *namban-ji* (literally, foreigners' or "southern barbarians'" temples), as the early Christian churches in Japan were called, are vague, contradictory, and few in number. A church built in Kyoto in 1569 and taken down in 1585 is known to have had a tile roof in irimoya style with a cross on top. It is also known that Father Gnecchi Organtino, in an audience with Nobunaga, received an offer of land for both a church and a house at Azuchi. Later, land was given in Kyoto for the construction of a Christian church. Such a structure, however, would undoubtedly have been torn down during Hideyoshi's proscription of the Christians in 1587. Still later, Ieyasu gave Father Rodriguez permission to build a church in Kyoto, but this also must have been torn down in 1614, when anti-Christian measures were once more strictly enforced. There are references to three or four other churches prior to 1614. Christian graves of the Momoyama period have been excavated in Kyoto, and a bell at the Shunko-in purports to have come from a namban-ji. It bears the date 1577 and the Christian monogram I.H.S. above a cross. We have no records of early church architecture except for a few vague representations on screens and one fan painting.

Temples and Shrines

Temple architecture in the Momoyama period consisted mostly of reconstructing buildings that had been destroyed in the preceding years of civil strife. Most of these structures were rebuilt according to their former plans, and thus new developments in form were hampered. Hideyoshi gave financial aid for the reconstruction of the Enryaku-ji on Mt. Hiei to the east of Kyoto, the Kongobu-ji on Mt. Koya, the Nishi Hongan-ji in Kyoto, and the Daigo-ji to the south of Fushimi. His son Hideyori aided in the restoration of the To-ji, the Nanzen-ji, and the Shokoku-ji in Kyoto, the Miidera in Otsu, the Hokke-ji in Nara Prefecture, and the Kongo-ji in Osaka Prefecture.

The Kodai-ji, built by Hideyoshi's widow in 1604, was one of the few temples created in the style of the period. The existing buildings display brightly lacquered pillars, colorful carved ornaments, and shining metal fittings. These buildings were connected by covered corridors, one of which, still intact at the Kodai-ji and known as the Ganryudo, is so constructed that its ascending roof resembles a dragon's back.

In shrine architecture of the Momoyama period, three styles developed. The *gongen* style is a combination of Buddhist and Shinto architecture in which the oratory and the sanctum are joined under one roof with the addition of a middle room. The *yatsumune* (eight-roof) style is a modification of this, with the addition of two wings and a very complicated roof plan such as that of the Kitano Shrine in Kyoto. Although the name of the style implies eight roofs, the number is actually variable. The Asama style, which derives its name from the example of the Asama Shrine in Shizuoka Prefecture, calls for a two-story main hall with a balcony on the upper floor. Shrines of the period were embellished with ornate decorations. Tsukubusama Shrine on Chikubu Island in Lake Biwa contains many brightly colored wood carvings representative of the era.

264. Kodai-ji.

265. Ganryudo, Kodai-ji.

266. Roof, Kitano Shrine.

267. Tsukubusama Shrine.

268. Railing Cap, Sanjo Bridge.

Sanjo Bridge

In 1589, Hideyoshi gave orders for the construction of a fine bridge across the Kamo River on Sanjo Street in Kyoto. This was not the first bridge on this busy road, but it is thought to have been the first Japanese bridge of any size to be supported by stone pillars. The *giboshi* or bronze railing caps from Hideyoshi's bridge are used on the present structure. Several of the original stone pillars from the Momoyama period can be seen today at each end of the present bridge, and remains of others are used as steppingstones in the garden of the Heian Shrine. When Kyoto was the capital of Japan, all distances were measured from the center of Sanjo Bridge.

The O-doi

In 1591, Hideyoshi ordered the construction of an earthen wall around the city of Kyoto. The main purpose seemed to be for defense, since guardhouses were located at the openings in the wall. This huge structure, with a moat on one or sometimes both sides, also served to mark the city boundaries. The capital in Heian times was surrounded by a fence, and it is also thought that the O-doi (Great Wall) was built in imitation of that of the early capital of Kyoto or its Chinese predecessor. The area enclosed was oblong in shape, with the longer section running from north to south. The Kamo River marked the eastern boundary. A great number of men must have been used for this work, for the whole construction job reportedly took only five months. Small sections of the O-doi can be seen today in northern Kyoto.

APPENDIX

A List of Other Noteworthy Examples of Momoyama Architecture

CASTLES

- Hikone Castle
- Himeji Castle
- Hirosaki Castle
- Hiroshima Castle (rebuilt)
- Kishiwada Castle
- Kumamoto Castle
- Maruoka Castle
- Matsue Castle
- Matsumoto Castle
- Okayama Castle
- Toyama Castle
- Ueno Castle
- Wakayama Castle (rebuilt)

SHOIN

- Furoshoin of Katsura Detached Palace, Kyoto City
- Kyakuden of Kangaku-in, Otsu City
- Kyakuden of Kojo-in, Otsu City
- Shinden of Emman-in, Otsu City

SUKIYA

- Gepparo of Katsura Detached Palace, Kyoto City
- Jo-an of Mitsui estate, Oiso City
- Oribe Hasso-an, Nara City
- Shonan-tei of Saiho-ji, Kyoto City
- Zangetsu-tei of Omote-Senke, Kyoto City

TEMPLES

- Hondo of Zuigen-ji, Miyazaki Prefecture
- Kaisando and Mitamaya of Kodai-ji, Kyoto City

SHRINES

- Asama Jinja, Shizuoka Prefecture
- Kitano Jinja, Kyoto City

Ozaki Hachiman Jinja, Sendai City
Tsukubusama Jinja, Chikubu Island, Lake Biwa

OTHER STRUCTURES FROM FUSHIMI CASTLE

Honden of Tsukubusama Jinja, Chikubu Island, Lake Biwa
Honden of Shoden-ji, Kyoto City
Kyakuden of Konchi-in, To-ji, Kyoto City
Kyakuden of Saikyo-ji, Sakamoto City

Short Bibliography

This bibliography is arranged by category rather than by language. Languages within an individual book other than that represented by the title are indicated in parentheses, as is other pertinent information.

ARCHITECTURAL SURVEYS

Drexler, Arthur: *The Architecture of Japan,* New York, 1955

Harada, Jiro: *The Lesson of Japanese Architecture,* London, 1954

Inoue, Kazuyuki: *Nihon Kenchiku Yoshiki,* Tokyo, 1954

Ota, Hirotaro; Tanabe, Tai; and Hattori, Katsukichi: *Nihon no Kenchiku,* Tokyo, 1953 (many large photographs with English captions and dates)

Paine, Robert Treat, and Soper, Alexander: *The Art and Architecture of Japan,* Harmondsworth, England, 1955

CASTLES

Fujioka, Michio: *Shiro to Jokamachi,* Tokyo, 1952

Guillain, Florent: *Châteaux-Forts Japonais,* Bulletin de la Maison Franco-Japonaise, Tome XIII, No. 1, Tokyo, 1941

Inoue, Munekazu: *Castles of Japan,* Tokyo, 1958 (short text and many large photographs)

Orui, Noboru: *Nihon no Shiro,* Tokyo, 1953

Orui, N., and Toba, M.: *Castles in Japan,* Tokyo, 1933

SHOIN

Kitao, Harumichi: *Shoin Architecture in Detailed Illustrations,* Tokyo, 1956 (line drawings and photographs plus captions in poor English)

SUKIYA

Emori, Nahiko, and Asahitani, Sau: *Chashitsu,* Osaka, 1949 (short introduction and table of contents in English)

Kitao, Harumichi: *Cha-no-Yu Houses in Detailed Illustrations,* Tokyo, 1953 (line drawings and photographs plus captions in poor English)

———: *Chashitsu Kenchiku,* Tokyo, 1956

———: *Sukiya Kenchiku Shizushu: Higashi Momoyama Jidai,* Tokyo, 1935 (text in English and Japanese)

Okakura, Kakuzo: *The Book of Tea,* Rutland, Vermont and Tokyo, 1958

Sadler, A. L.: *Cha-no-Yu: The Japanese Tea Ceremony,* Tokyo, 1933

PAINTING

Doru, Tsuguyoshi: *Momoyama Shohekiga no Kansho,* Tokyo, 1943

Paine, Robert Treat, and Soper, Alexander: *The Art and Architecture of Japan,* Harmondsworth, England, 1955

Society of Friends of Eastern Art: *Index of Japanese Painters,* Tokyo, 1958

Tanaka, Ichimatsu: *Momoyama no Bi,* Tokyo, 1957 (introduction and list of plates in English)

HISTORIES OF FUSHIMI, KYOTO, AND THE MOMOYAMA PERIOD

Boxer, C. R.: *The Christian Century in Japan, 1549–1650,* Tokyo, 1955

Dening, Walter: *The Life of Toyotomi Hideyoshi,* Tokyo, 1955 (a combination of history and legend)

Fane, Ponsonby: *Kyoto,* Hong Kong, 1931

Kato, Jiro: *Fushimi Momoyama no Bunkashi,* Tokyo, 1953

Okabe, Seiichi, ed.: *Azuchi Momoyama Jidai Shi,* Tokyo, 1915

Sadler, A. L.: *The Maker of Modern Japan: The Life of Tokugawa Ieyasu,* London, 1937

Tsukamoto, Tetsuji, ed.: *Taikoki,* Tokyo, 1919

Index

NOTE: Numbers in italics indicate pages on which illustrations appear. Long marks for Japanese vowels, although omitted in the text, are given in index entries.